CREDITS

1732011

191984

221084

AUX SYS

SYSTEM DESIGN
NATHAN DOWDELL

LINE DEVELOPMENT
SAM WEBB

WRITING
JIM JOHNSON, NATHAN DOWDELL,
AND AARON POLLYEA

CANON EDITING
SCOTT PEARSON

EDITING
MIKE BRUNTON, SAM WEBB,
AND JIM JOHNSON

PROOFREADING
ARIC WIEDER

COVER ARTWORK
ELI MAFFEI

INTERNAL ARTWORK
RODRIGO GONZALEZ, CONNOR MAGILL,
WAYNE MILLER, GRZEGORZ PEDRYCZ,
ÁNGEL ALONSO MIGUEL, MARTIN SOBR,
JACK KASIER, NICK GREENWOOD,
DOUG DREXLER, TOBIAS RICHTER,
MICHAL E. CROSS, DAVID METLESITS,
MICHELE FRIGO, CRISTI BALANESCU,
AND JOSEPH DIAZ

ART DIRECTION
SAM WEBB AND JIM JOHNSON

GRAPHIC DESIGN
MATTHEW COMBEN

LAYOUT
MICHAL E. CROSS AND RICHARD L. GALE

INDEX BY
BILL HERON

PRODUCED BY
CHRIS BIRCH

PUBLISHING ASSISTANT
SALWA AZAR

OPERATIONS MANAGER
GARRY HARPER

PRODUCTION MANAGER
STEVE DALDRY

COMMUNITY SUPPORT
LLOYD GYAN

FOR CBS STUDIOS
JOHN VAN CITTERS, MARIAN CORDRY,
VERONICA HART, AND KEITH LOWENADLER

MŌDIPHIÜS™
ENTERTAINMENT
2D20™

Published by Modiphius Entertainment Ltd.
2nd Floor, 39 Harwood Road, London, SW6 4QP, England.
Printed by GrafikMediaProduktionsmanagement GmbH

INFO@MODIPHIUS.COM
WWW.MODIPHIUS.COM
STARTREK.COM

Modiphius Entertainment Product Number: MUH051063
ISBN: 978-1-910132-87-6

CONTENTS

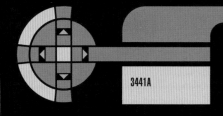

3441A

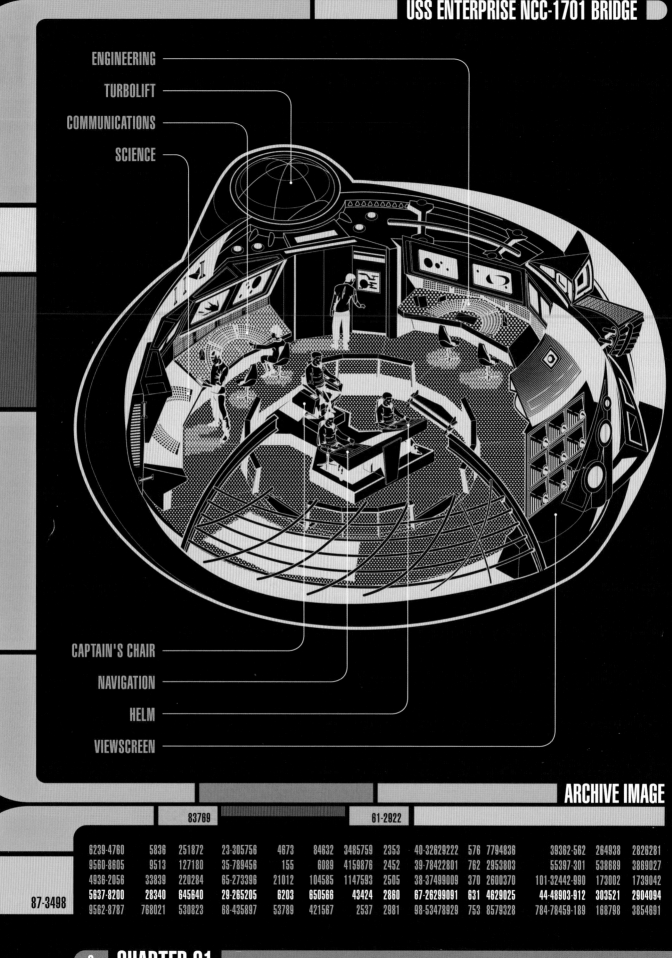

ENGINEERING

TURBOLIFT

COMMUNICATIONS

SCIENCE

CAPTAIN'S CHAIR

NAVIGATION

HELM

VIEWSCREEN

ARCHIVE IMAGE

83769

61-2922

	6239-4760	5836	251872	23-305756	4673	84632	3485759	2353	40-32629222	576	7794836	39362-562	264938	2826281
	9560-8605	9513	127180	35-789456	155	6089	4159876	2452	39-78422801	762	2953803	55397-301	538689	3869027
	4936-2056	33839	220284	65-273396	21012	104585	1147593	2505	38-37499009	370	2600370	101-32442-990	173002	1739042
87-3498	5637-8200	28340	645640	29-265205	6203	650566	43424	2860	67-26299091	631	4629025	44-48903-912	303521	2904094
	9562-8787	768021	530823	68-435897	53789	421567	2537	2981	98-53478929	753	8579328	784-78459-189	168798	3854691

CHAPTER 01.00

INTRODUCTION

35204572030026
40360555022

INTRODUCTION
LEAD BY EXAMPLE

"YOU'RE THE CAPTAIN OF THIS SHIP. YOU HAVEN'T THE RIGHT TO BE VULNERABLE IN THE EYES OF THE CREW. YOU CAN'T AFFORD THE LUXURY OF BEING ANYTHING LESS THAN PERFECT. IF YOU DO, THEY LOSE FAITH AND YOU LOSE COMMAND."

— COMMANDER SPOCK

From "wet" navies to modern Starfleet, beings across the Galaxy have voyaged in command of ships of wood, steel, duranium, and much else. With their own grasp on the tiller or someone else at the helm, ship captains and pilots have existed as long as there have been ships to navigate.

While not all cadets dream of life aboard a starship, command of a starship is the target for exceptional cadets. This is the dream of many in the Alpha and Beta Quadrants, and only the brightest and boldest of Starfleet officers make it. Command of a Starfleet starship is an honor that requires a broad range of skills and abilities as well as boldness and courage, and a person capable of dealing with Starfleet personnel and civilians at all levels.

A captain is required to be a diplomat, a Federation lawyer, a disaster-response manager, and a tactician. They must know preliminary first contact procedures. A captain is encouraged to take science and engineering courses, not to mention as-needed training so that they can support the duties of all the personnel under them. Due to the exhaustive skills required to earn a captaincy, many Starfleet captains serve for years in lesser roles and in other departments before transferring to command.

Modern technology is a marvelous fusion of science and engineering, but every vessel requires an officer at the controls. Starfleet officers with great vision, reflexes, and a steady hand aspire to become pilots of the great explorer vessels, the *Nova*, *Intrepid*, and *Galaxy*-class starships, as well as all the various other classes and support vessels. Zipping in and out of gaseous anomalies in a runabout, pushing the envelope in an experimental Starfleet short-range fighter, taking the helm of a behemoth like an *Olympic*-class vessel: these are times when the captain and crew are happiest knowing there's someone other than a computer at the helm.

Command division officers, like other Starfleet officers, may come from any walk of life, planet, background or circumstances. A cadet's background may have a small bearing on entry and success within the command track at the Academy but, ultimately, your pedigree doesn't matter once you get to the Academy. The instructors know how to separate the true commanders from the rest. It's no reflection on anyone if they're unable to complete command-level courses and exercises. It takes an officer with the right mix of skills and personality to succeed as a commander of one of Starfleet's prized and precious starships.

YESTERDAY'S ENTERPRISE

While the default year of **Star Trek Adventures** is 2371 (Stardates 48000-48999), all other *Star Trek* eras are available if desired by the Gamemaster and Players. For the command division, little has changed since Archer's and Kirk's eras, other than uniform color from gold to red, an adjustment in ranks used in Starfleet, the unification of the 23rd century roles helmsman and navigator into the conn role, and the types of starships and support craft to be piloted.

Gamemasters wishing to run missions during other time periods will have no trouble using information and rules in this sourcebook. If a game rule, item of equipment, or technological advance is not available in a certain era (transporters, replicators, holodecks, etc.) there will be a sidebar like this one.

Likewise, earning an assignment as the conn officer aboard a starship takes talent not every boomer, bush pilot, or skimmer jockey can claim. There are countless instances in Starfleet's history where a starship was saved or lost solely on the ability of its helmsman or conn officer. Commanding a starship takes a certain fearless personality, and piloting one through the countless varieties of interstellar phenomena requires an individual every bit as daring. The captain is in charge of the well-being of the ship and crew; the conn officer is responsible for getting the ship's crew to their next destination and mission.

While Starfleet boasts an officer corps with the best and brightest people the Federation has to offer, it can be argued that the members of Starfleet's command division are a cut above "ordinary" Starfleet officers or, if not above, then cast in a slightly different mold. A sciences department head and a chief engineer may be exemplary officers and leaders in their own right, but it's still the captain of the ship the crew looks to for inspiration, support and, in many cases, hope when facing the incredible odds Starfleet officers accept as part of their daily duty.

CAPTAIN'S PERSONAL LOG

STARDATE 48224.9

Today was... amazing. And humbling. I've been working toward this moment my entire career, and here it is. I was piped aboard the *U.S.S. Dunbar* at 0930 hours and the next eleven hours were just fantastic.

I had to hide my enthusiasm, of course. I couldn't let my excitement show too much for my new crew. Had to show the captain was a rock of confidence and strength. I hope I carried it well.

The meeting with the senior staff, rather, MY senior staff, also went well. Even though I only knew two of them personally, I think I made the right calls on all the other positions, especially my XO. Commander Tes and I seem to mesh well together and I think we're going to be a good team. That may be first day optimism clouding my judgement, but she's a fine officer and a sage leader, and I think I'll learn a lot from her and her symbiote's long years in the service.

I'm exhausted, but ecstatic. The first walk through the ship was long, but well worth it. I need to follow up with Ch'Kull, my chief engineer, and figure out why the port impulse engine is acting up. Other than that, the ship is ready for our first mission together. I can't wait to get underway. End personal log entry.

EVERY OPPORTUNITY

Viceroy Killeen,

Thank you for the letter of recommendation regarding your daughter. Also, thank you for the delightful package of assorted Acadian chocolates: you are clearly better informed then I could have ever guessed. However, please find returned with this message the deposit datarod you sent which was connected to a truly generous quantity of gold-pressed latinum. Your world is relatively new to the Federation, so I'll simply say your generosity was not required.

Starfleet is based on competency, not currency. Postings are not purchased but are earned through the hard work, sweat, tears, and sacrifices of those called to command. Your daughter comes highly recommended as a command branch candidate. Even without the monetary inducement, Taila will receive every opportunity to excel at tasks and exercises designed to determine if she is capable of leading a crew of officers into danger and coming out on top.

I've had the good fortune to speak with your daughter at length, and I'm absolutely comfortable extending my recommendation for Academy admission. She will bring great pride to you and your people should she complete training and accept a Starfleet commission.

Respectfully,
Admiral Jared Locke, Starbase 224

CONTENTS OF THIS BOOK

This Command Division supplement provides Gamemasters and Players with a wealth of information on Starfleet's command division. The command and conn departments are covered in detail including historical information on each, their purposes in Starfleet, the duties of each, and career paths for individuals in either department. This book also provides new and expanded rules for Social Conflict, additional Focuses and Talents, and a wealth of new lifepath options and career enhancements for command division Player Characters.

CHAPTER 2: COMMAND DIVISION

The command division plays a critical role within Starfleet, at all levels of the service, and on every starship, starbase, outpost, and other Starfleet facility or vessel. This chapter provides details on the command division's purpose in Starfleet and explains the key roles played by officers and enlisted personnel wearing the red uniform. The structure of Starfleet Command is examined in detail, along with how Starfleet Command affects every division of Starfleet.

Fleet Operations, a key part of a commander's life, is also detailed in this chapter. This section discusses operations, deployments, and the role starbases play in fleet deployments and ship assignments. Details on Starfleet Command's legal arm, the Judge Advocate General's Office, are provided, along with discussions of

courts-martial, the Prime Directive and how these impact a command officer.

Most command officers start at Starfleet Academy, and this chapter specifically focuses on cadets who display an aptitude for command and a leadership disposition. Those cadets who possess a steady hand on the tiller and eyes like an eagle — both the hallmarks of an elite pilot — are discussed as well.

Since it's likely that most of your *Star Trek Adventures* will take place aboard a starship, a detailed account of starship operations is also included, discussing the role of commanding officers in running a ship and crew, as well as information on starship, station, and outpost duty watches.

CHAPTER 3: COMMAND DIVISION CHARACTERS

This chapter focuses on Player Character options for command division characters, and expands on the mechanics in the core rulebook. Options for new Player ranks from Commodore to Fleet Admiral are provided, with advice for creating characters for the command department on board a starship or starbase. An expanded list of Focuses and Talents within the Command Discipline, from leadership and diplomatic abilities to tactical training, is provided.

This chapter also looks at officers in the conn position, including the training necessary to control a starship or smaller craft, and conn's role in both regular ship operations and combat. There is advice for the conn Player on how to make the most of their role. A list of new Focuses and Talents for the Conn Discipline, from navigation and combat maneuvers to warp travel, is provided.

This chapter expands the 2D20 Social Conflict rules to enhance diplomatic encounters during a game session.

LETTER TO HOME

Blessed Mother and Father,

I trust this letter finds you both healthy and hearty. Carina told me that the winter brought heavy snow to much of the New Caledonia colony. I'd like to say I miss the snow there but, honestly, there are peaks on Earth that just dwarf those back home. Not that I've had a lot of time to play in the snow — my course load and extra seat time has consumed my life.

Mother, you'll be amused to know that I talk about you frequently with my fellow pilot cadets. They can barely believe the stories I tell of how you used to fly me around as a child in the old propeller-driven biplane you and Grandmama cobbled together. They're all used to holodecks and holosuites and fake experiences. None of them seem to have the engineering knowledge to consider building a plane for themselves!

And I have to thank you, Mother, for reminding me how challenging Academy pilot courses would be. I've learned more about astronomy, astronavigation, and starship protocols in the last four weeks than I thought existed. How you managed to keep it all straight during your years in Starfleet is beyond me!

Father, I wanted you to know that I took your advice and reached out to senior cadet T'Perr. He did recognize me from the Vulcan survey mission to our colony and has agreed to give me counseling on leadership principles from a Vulcan perspective. He was emphatic that he would not show any favoritism, but I think what he can teach me will help a lot if I decide to try for a place in Nova Squadron.

Please extend my love to the elders of the town, and know that I carry you both in my heart and soul every day.

Love,
Mitchell

INTERCEPTED ROMULAN INTELLIGENCE REPORT

Senator, appended to this letter is the report of my first undercover year aboard the Federation Starbase 157. It includes my findings after speaking to many Starfleet officers and Federation citizens while in service here.

One thing I wish to particularly point out is my recommendation that you encourage the Tal Shiar to step up their plans to infiltrate Starfleet Academy and plant an operative as a cadet. Given what I have seen of the personnel coming out of Starfleet Academy, we should make every effort to investigate their training regimen and find out how they are creating their officers.

I do not doubt the capabilities of our officers but what I have seen from Starfleet is astonishing. I stole a recent after-action report of an encounter along the Neutral Zone, and it detailed an engagement between one of our top-line Warbirds and a Federation *Nebula*-class vessel. While the Warbird is superior in every way, from power level to weaponry, defensive systems, and maneuverability, the *Nebula*-class vessel somehow managed to outshine our vessel and literally run laps around it as the two ships chased each other in and around the Cara'bree asteroid field. Given their technological inferiority, I have to surmise that their crew was the superior. If our adversary fields inferior equipment with superior officers and still defeats us, we certainly need to figure out how to correct our personnel deficiencies.

Respectfully,
Subcommander Nevet

CHAPTER 4: FEDERATION STARSHIPS

This chapter provides details on 24 Federation vessels from all *Star Trek* eras. The vessels supplement the Spaceframes found in the core rulebook, give the Gamemaster a wealth of starship options on which to base a campaign or series, and provide Players with a number of craft to pilot through the cosmos.

CHAPTER 5: USING THE COMMAND DIVISION

This chapter helps the Gamemaster focus on command and conn Player Characters in action. It provides additional tools and storylines for diplomatic encounters, negotiations, and legalities, and other command- and conn-oriented scenarios. It also includes a discussion of mission structure, and missions for command and conn officers. Special attention is given to the challenge with giving orders in a game and how a Player Character captain, executive officer, and senior officers

(department heads) should treat bridge crew Player Characters, and Player Characters or NPCs on their department staffs. It provides guidance on how a Player Character can develop department staff NPCs with the Gamemaster's support.

It also gives guidance on developing missions and stories built around command and conn officers, including first contact missions, the Prime Directive, the Judiciary or Judge Advocate Generals Office, and how command division officers might find themselves embroiled in a conspiracy. Also included are rules for an Admiralty-level campaign or series of missions where Players are responsible for fleet-scale conflict.

CHAPTER 6: COMMAND DIVISION NON-PLAYER CHARACTERS

This chapter provides detailed descriptions and game statistics for a range of command and conn oriented NPCs to use as allies or adversaries.

COUNSELING SESSION 2, CADET HOULE

(PARTIAL TRANSCRIPT)

Cadet Houle: Well, I don't know, Counselor. I mean, command was my dream for, for ever. I was meant to wear that red uniform.

Counselor Dyre: And how do you feel about remaining in operations?

Cadet Houle: Well, awful, honestly. How does standing at a tactical station or walking patrol get me closer to commanding a starship?

Counselor Dyre: It's good to have goals and ambitions. But… I've reviewed your Academy record. How do you feel your accomplishments and challenges at the Academy impacted your posting outside of a command role?

Cadet Houle: Part of it has to be my performance on the *Maru* exercise. I kinda left everyone on the deck in that one.

Counselor Dyre: Most, nearly all, cadets fail that particular exercise, at least from a mission standpoint. It's a test of character, not of your ability to beat an impossible mission.

Cadet Houle: I have character. I did score well on the test.

Counselor Dyre: You did. It was just one factor...

Cadet Houle: I suppose. I didn't expect my off-duty shore leave activities would reflect on my Academy records or on my first assignment, though.

Counselor Dyre: <laughs> Yes, well, Starfleet has to evaluate the entire cadet, not just what they see in the classroom or in exercises. Especially for a command role or an eventual starship commission.

It's one thing to talk about being a commander… and another to live and act in that role.

Cadet Houle: Are you saying I need to act like a captain when I'm off duty?

Counselor Dyre: If you want that role badly enough, you should consider acting like it all the time, especially off duty. A starship captain rarely has the luxury of off-duty time. While they do have a senior staff to handle the day-to-day running of the ship and crew, the captain may be called on to handle a crisis at literally any moment. That potential stress is one not everyone can handle. We can teach some skills, but much has to come from a person's inherent nature and life experiences.

Cadet Houle: I guess. Yeah.

Counselor Dyre: Take heart, Cadet. Most Starfleet captains reached the center seat after years in a variety of roles, and gained valuable experience working up the ranks and learning from everyone in the chain of command. Your marks at the Academy were in the top 10th percentile… You've been posted to a good ship with a good captain and executive officer. If you apply yourself as admirably as you conducted your Academy years, I expect you'll be a department head in a few years and ready for the bridge officer training programs.

Cadet Houle: So, you suggest steady growth and development?

Counselor Dyre: Indeed, I do.

CHAPTER 02.00 COMMAND DIVISION

34362070473892
12849304474

COMMAND DIVISION
DEPARTMENTS

"A STARSHIP CAPTAIN IS NOT MANUFACTURED — HE, OR SHE, IS BORN FROM INSIDE — FROM THE CHARACTER OF THE INDIVIDUAL..."

— SIRNA KOLRAMI

BRIEFING

All right, captain. As a refresher let's cover the basics about Starfleet's divisions. As any Academy cadet knows, officers and enlisted personnel within Starfleet wear one of three colors: red for the command division, blue for sciences, and gold for operations. Each division has has two broad departments. This briefing will cover the command division and its command and conn departments. Command is for commanders and captains: officers destined for a starship center seat, and all flag-level officers. The conn department is for officers who pilot support craft, shuttles, and starships in addition to their other duties.

THE COMMAND DEPARTMENT

Command department officers are found on all Starfleet starships, starbases, and other facilities. The commander aboard will almost always be from the command department, although there are exceptions: a sciences officer may command a science research station; a tactical officer might head a deep-space listening post; or a medical officer could supervise an emergency disaster recovery center. But by and large, you see an admiral, captain, or commander in charge of a starship or starbase — all are command department personnel.

The command department, as part of the command division, is the department tasked primarily with interpreting and executing Starfleet orders, directives, and policy to support the Federation Council's orders and directives. Starfleet is the exploratory and defensive arm of the Federation Council. It does not normally conduct operations without the Council's approval. While the Federation Council creates the policy and parameters within which Starfleet operates, it's the flag and line officers who enact those policies and parameters on the frontier and out in the field.

The command department is the connective tissue between the Federation Council and a crew, with the captain acting as the conduit for the Council's will and crew's actions, all in the service of Starfleet and the Federation.

Command department officers consist of all flag-rank officers (admirals), most captains, and any commanders or lower ranks that are assigned to the command department. Almost all Starfleet vessels are commanded by a captain in the command department, though there are some, such as dedicated science vessels and vessels assigned to Starfleet's Corps of Engineers, that are commanded by ranked captains of the relevant department. Sometimes highly experienced officers within a non-command department are promoted to captain or above, such as retired Captain Montgomery Scott, or the director of Starfleet Medical who may be a commander, captain, or an admiral from the sciences or medical departments.

THE CONN DEPARTMENT

At first blush, the conn department might seem to be the slightly unloved "red-headed stepchild" of the division, even though its personnel wear the red command uniform. Appearances are wrong. Conn officers are the most common Starfleet personnel encountered by Federation officials; conn officers pilot every form of starship, shuttle, runabout, skimmer, and other support craft at almost every Federation facility.

Conn officers are, perhaps, the most cross-trained officers in Starfleet. Their primary posting is aboard a starship, manning the helm or conn on the bridge, so each must be trained in a wide variety of sciences and skills, including astronomy, astronavigation, stellar cartography, assorted space sciences, complex mathematics, proper operation of not only the conn but every other bridge station. And then there's their ability to repair the ships, shuttles, and systems under

their control. Good conn officers are an incredible fusion of engineering, sciences, and operations.

Commissioned conn officers tend to be ensigns, junior grade lieutenants, and few full lieutenants. There are very few lieutenant commanders, and no commanders or captains in the role. The primary reason conn officers tend to be young and lower ranked is indirectly due to their cross-training. A tour of duty or two at the conn gives an officer invaluable bridge experience, and the opportunity to manage other bridge stations. These young officers are exposed to operations tasks, tactical maneuvers, science observations, and engineering feats. All that experience provides opportunities for conn officers to transfer to every other bridge station. And then there's their ability to repair.

Non-commissioned officers within the conn department perform critical tasks in support of the commissioned officers aboard a ship or starbase. They may serve as shuttle pilots working the standard Starfleet supply routes, act as logistics officers at starbases or outposts, or serve as a personal pilot for an Admiral or government official. Experienced non-coms also stand occasional bridge duty watches or act as back-up conn officers during Red Alerts.

RANK AND POSITION

One aspect of Starfleet that causes confusion to those not familiar with a traditional navy or Starfleet itself is what the difference is between a captain's rank and a captain posting. "Captain" is a rank someone achieves during their career, usually indicating successful time in progressively more challenging positions of ever-increasing responsibility. This is linked to an officer's gradually increasing skillset and capability to lead. Earning the fourth gold rank pip of a captain is an achievement few Starfleet officers achieve.

Quite separate from the fleet's rank structure and chain of command, the position of captain has, since the days of sailing vessels, been the traditional term given to anyone in charge of a boat or ship. They are always the vessel's captain.

Because the role is separate from rank, it is possible to have the captain of a Starfleet vessel not be a captain. Some Starfleet vessels, such as scout ships and light cruisers (the *Saber* class, for example), may have a commander as the captain instead of a full captain. In rare cases, a highly-qualified lieutenant commander may be in post as the captain of a small starship. Usually, though, the captain of a Starfleet vessel also happens to carry the rank of captain.

Enlisted officers (non-commissioned officers, "non-coms", or NCOs) serve in critical roles in every department and branch of Starfleet. Enlistment is for individuals who wish to serve in Starfleet without attending the Academy in a role with less responsibility. Unlike Academy-trained commissioned officers, enlisted personnel serve a single tour of duty, with an option to remain in Starfleet for additional tours.

There are enlisted Starfleet personnel who have served longer than many officers and they are highly sought after, being as valuable as any qualified executive officer. Having an experienced, knowledgeable NCO crewmember aboard a ship is a significant asset no captain will easily give up.

CHAPTER 02.20

COMMAND DIVISION
STARFLEET COMMAND

HEADQUARTERS

Starfleet Command headquarters is in San Francisco on Earth. Within that umbrella title are numerous branches, departments, levels of command, and organizations. The bureaucracy inside Starfleet is too large a topic to delve into here, so this is a brief overview of the key pieces with the focus on the most important parts.

COMMANDER-IN-CHIEF

The commander-in-chief of Starfleet has always been, and is, the current president of the Federation. Starfleet exists to serve the president's requirements to enforce Federation laws; to defend Federation citizens, assets, and territories; and to perform any other task the president requires, within Federation law and with the approval of the Federation Council.

The president works with the Federation Council and Starfleet's joint chiefs to develop Starfleet policy and mission parameters. While the president sets the tone for Starfleet's direction, they do not manage operations on a day-to-day basis. The president is far too busy, and Starfleet is only one piece of the larger Federation government.

THE JOINT CHIEFS

A panel of admirals manages Starfleet's day-to-day operations, each the chief officer of one of Starfleet's major branches, some of which are discussed shortly. The panel changes as the requirements of Starfleet change from administration to administration. Each chief has decades of experience, and they are the most able officers within Starfleet ranks. The president of the Federation nominates new joint chiefs when an opening on the panel appears, though the Federation Council interviews all candidates and ratifies nominations. The joint chiefs report to both the Federation Council (through the Security Council) and the Federation president.

The joint chiefs meet regularly to discuss starship assignments, fleet deployments, personnel issues, scientific research requirements, humanitarian or disaster relief actions, and any other activity that involves Starfleet assets or personnel. When there is a conflict of interest or multiple needs for the same Starfleet resources (for example, Research & Exploration needing a starship to investigate a new spatial anomaly in the same sector as a plague outbreak that requires Starfleet Medical resources), the joint chiefs resolve the matter. Once policies and missions have been agreed to, they solicit approval from

...he president and the Council, except when time is of the essence and lives are at stake.

Let's look at the branches of Starfleet which are commonly connected to a captain's career.

FLEET OPERATIONS

"Fleet Ops" is the Starfleet branch most directly involved in standard mission assignments and personnel management. This branch receives orders from the joint chiefs and assigns fleets and individual starships to carry out those orders. Once Fleet Operations has decided on a course of action, orders flow down to fleet and sector admirals as appropriate, though there have been cases where a time-sensitive mission has been assigned directly to a captain and crew by Fleet Ops.

Other branches within Starfleet may issue requests to Fleet Ops when there is a need for a starship and crew to perform a task that does not directly relate to orders from the chain of command. For example, the Diplomatic Corps is negotiating a non-aggression pact with a newly-encountered species when matters go unexpectedly sideways; they then need the nearest starship to show the flag and provide support. In this instance, the Diplomatic Corps would send a priority request to Fleet Ops, which would then, with the relevant fleet or sector admiral, review the list of nearby ships and assign the appropriate one to a support mission.

Fleet Operations maintains a situational awareness of the location and disposition of all Starfleet vessels and crews, and ensures that all Federation worlds, protectorates, and other interests are defended or within range of a starship. Some of the smaller branches of the service under Fleet Ops include: the Corps of Engineers; the Judge Advocate General's Office; Starbase Operations, which is responsible for deep space stations, outposts, sensor arrays, and other such facilities in addition to starbases; and Shipyard Operations. We'll talk about Fleet Ops in more detail shortly.

RESEARCH AND DEVELOPMENT

Next to Fleet Ops, Research and Development (or R&D) is arguably the most important branch of Starfleet. There is an ongoing argument in the Federation Council that R&D should be the primary branch of Starfleet: the fleet, according to some, should be focused on exploration and research, and not on militaristic activities such as border patrols, convoy escorts, and "fleet posturing".

R&D is responsible for all Starfleet's scientific and exploration efforts from planetary surveys and anomaly investigation to charting new star clusters. R&D is also responsible for medical research conducted by Starfleet personnel, and is often the first branch to be consulted when a new plague is discovered. R&D has a few starships under its direct control focused entirely on scientific research of one sort or another.

The Starfleet Medical *Olympic*-class vessels also belong to R&D, though they are often reassigned based upon the needs of Fleet Ops or the joint chiefs. There are dozens of smaller branches within R&D, including one for each of the major space sciences (planetary, astronomical, etc.) and, in coordination with the Corps of Engineers, the Advanced Research branch, an elite think tank.

FLAG OFFICERS IN 2371

A selection of admirals currently serving in Starfleet and whom you may encounter during your career:

- **Vice Admiral Anthony Haftel:** Haftel is a flag officer specializing in cybernetics and is assigned to Starfleet's Advanced Research division.

- **Admiral Alynna Nechayev:** Nechayev spent a number of years assigned to the Federation-Cardassian border and was influential in managing Starfleet's policy regarding Cardassia and Cardassian military operations.

- **Admiral Owen Paris:** Paris is an experienced Admiral well-versed in deep space communications technologies. He is currently a survival strategies instructor at Starfleet Academy.

- **Admiral William Ross:** Ross is one of Starfleet's more talented tactical flag officers and has been outspoken about the new Dominion threat.

- **Admiral T'Lara:** A Vulcan flag officer with a long career in Starfleet, T'Lara is the highest-ranking Vulcan flag officer currently in Starfleet.

THE DIPLOMATIC CORPS

Starfleet's Diplomatic Corps works with the Federation's Department of Interplanetary Affairs to manage current and potential diplomatic events. Starfleet crews are often the first on the scene for a first contact situation or other diplomatic event between the Federation and another culture. They must manage affairs to support Federation law and interests until a dedicated Starfleet or Federation diplomat arrives. The Diplomatic Corps provides training for Starfleet officers in negotiation, diplomacy, and first contact etiquette.

The Diplomatic Corps creates and revises orders and guidelines for many situations, including first contact procedures and best practices, colonization programs and procedures, and trade and treaty negotiations. Diplomatic Corps members are usually assigned to a starbase, and then sent into the field only for specific tasks. Some starships and their crews are dedicated to diplomatic affairs, and have a Diplomatic Corps member assigned to the ship.

FLEET ADMIRALS

Fleet admirals are just below the joint chiefs in Starfleet's chain of command. Each is responsible for a large section of space comprising several sectors, and a fleet Admiral's responsibilities may include dozens of starbases, starships, and all the personnel and support structure of a fleet. Fleet admirals act as the pipeline between the joint chiefs' mission requirements and the sector admirals who pass those requirements down to individual captains.

FLAG OFFICERS THROUGHOUT HISTORY

A selection of admirals, representing some of the highs and lows of Starfleet's history.

- **Vice Admiral Maxwell Forrest:** The architect of the NX Project in the mid 2100s, Forrest was one of the first Starfleet admirals and directly involved in the missions of the first *Enterprise*, NX-01. In 2154, after years of service, Forrest made the ultimate sacrifice defending Vulcan Ambassador Soval from a terrorist attack on Vulcan.

- **Fleet Admiral Cartwright:** While he served Starfleet with distinction throughout the mid- to late-23rd century — including an heroic effort to defend Earth during the probe

encounter of 2286 — Cartwright's earlier career has been overshadowed by his criminal involvement in the 2293 conspiracy. He plotted to assassinate the Federation President and thereby sabotage the Klingon-Federation peace talks. Cartwright was tried and dishonorably discharged.

- **Rear Admiral James T. Kirk:** One of Starfleet's most renowned captains, Kirk was promoted to admiral in the early 2270s and served as Chief of Starfleet Operations. His career as an admiral was effective, though he often expressed a desire to return to starship command. After the V'Ger incident, the battle with Khan Noonien Singh, and the resolution of the space probe encounter, Kirk was demoted to Captain and assigned to the *U.S.S. Enterprise*-A.

- **Vice Admiral J.P. Hansen:** A career tactical officer, Hansen was placed in charge of weapons and defenses R&D to combat the Borg menace. In 2367, he was killed in action by the Borg during the Battle of Wolf 359.

A captain and starship may be assigned to one region of space for one or more extended tours of duty, which means serving under the same fleet admiral for years. While Starfleet encourages individual starships to be assigned to a broad range of sectors, missions, and commanding officers, flag officers do note any special relationship a captain and crew have with a given planet or region, and try to keep such valuable assets under their command.

SECTOR ADMIRALS

The next rung down in Starfleet's structure are the sector admirals. They are responsible for one particular sector of space and all the Starfleet assets in that sector. Not all Federation sectors have a sector admiral; some are not sufficiently populated or explored, and therefore are the responsibility of a fleet admiral. Most sector admirals are posted to a starbase, though some fly their flag from a starship in a particular sector. This usually occurs in expansion sectors where the Federation has yet to establish a significant presence, or doesn't yet operate an outpost or starbase.

Starships may be assigned to one sector of space for a period of time. When this happens, captains report directly to the sector admiral unless otherwise directed. The sector admiral is the link to the Starfleet chain of command and the source of Starfleet orders.

FLEET CAPTAINS

While the role of fleet captain (the old, disused rank of commodore) is rarely needed any more, except during times of open warfare, it's worth looking at the duties of a fleet captain. This is not a rank, but a position that a captain may be given when a sector or fleet admiral needs a subordinate to lead a flotilla of a few starships working in concert. For example, if a sector admiral needed a small group of starships to ferret out pirates in a small region of space, one senior captain would oversee and direct the other captains and their ships. Once the mission is concluded, the flotilla disbands, the fleet captain loses his authority, and the vessels can be reassigned as needed as per normal Starfleet doctrine and practice.

CHAPTER
02.30

COMMAND DIVISION
FLEET OPERATIONS

THE ROLE OF FLEET OPERATIONS

As mentioned earlier, Fleet Operations is the branch of Starfleet involved in many Player Character activities. Nearly all orders come from Fleet Ops (and from the joint chiefs) through the fleet and sector admirals to the captains. Since Fleet Ops is such an integral part of Starfleet as a whole, it is worthwhile going into more detail.

Fleet Operations is responsible for keeping track of the location and disposition of all Starfleet vessels and crews, and ensures all Federation interests are sufficiently defended or at least within easy range of a starship. Because Federation holdings and interests in the Alpha and Beta Quadrants and beyond are constantly expanding, Fleet Ops, and therefore Starfleet, is constantly challenged to cover contingencies properly. One world's demand for Federation starships to patrol a shipping lane means another world may not have a starship within reach.

These demands require a delicate balancing act, one that the staff assigned to Fleet Ops wrestle with on an ongoing basis.

Fleet Ops maintains detailed records on every Starfleet starship and every Starfleet officer. For starships, Fleet Ops collects and analyzes maintenance schedules and results, armament stores and usage reports, power distribution, formal and informal mission logs, scientific research, crew rotation schedules, and duty watch logs. Records maintained for personnel include official ship logs, select unclassified personal logs, sanitized medical transcripts, training and educational transcripts, scenario results, and many more.

The reason Fleet Ops collects, analyzes, and stores so many records is because data is powerful. The more data Fleet Ops has on the daily operations of Starfleet's ships and crews, the better Starfleet can optimize their efforts. Countless procedures and guidelines have been developed based on the data gathered by Fleet Ops, so the seemingly-endless paperwork (even though no paper is used) required to complete for each duty watch and each mission does contribute, ultimately, to a more efficient Starfleet.

There are several key Starfleet branches under Fleet Ops. We'll discuss the more important ones in subsequent briefings, but it's also worth discussing how Fleet Ops manages fleet structure and deployments throughout the Alpha and Beta Quadrants. This will give a sense of how a single starship fits into the overall deployment structure of the entire fleet.

FLEET DEPLOYMENTS

Every starship in Starfleet, except those assigned to specific departments or classified missions, is assigned to a fleet of which there are three primary types: standing, mobile, and supporting.

Standing fleets are permanently assigned to one starbase or one region of space. While starships may be added or removed from a standing fleet, the fleet itself remains on station unless Federation policy requires a redeployment. For example, the First Fleet is assigned to Sector 001 where it patrols and defends Earth, the seat of the Federation Council and Starfleet Command.

Mobile fleets are focused on a specific mission type and are not tied to a specific location. These include any fleet sent to a crisis area and any fleet on deep-space exploration and research that isn't specifically tied to one exploration region. For example, the Eighth Fleet is assigned to an area including the Federation-Klingon border; it is tasked with the exploration of the Beta Quadrant beyond the boundaries of the Federation and Klingon Empire. Since this is a very large volume of space, the Eighth Fleet's mandate is broad and does not contain a fixed point of coordination. The three starships assigned to Starbase 364 (Narendra Station) and tasked with exploring the Shackleton Expanse are part of Eighth Fleet. It's possible that they will be transferred to another fleet based out of Narendra Station in the future.

Supporting fleets are nominally placed on standby status and are only used in times of crisis or specific need. They might be a disaster recovery fleet, a medical fleet, a colonization fleet, or an evacuation fleet. These are dispatched to complete a specific mission or task, and then return to their home port to repair and resupply before the next time they're used.

Depending upon the orders of the admiral in command, a fleet may be broken down in to 'groups' of ships dedicated to a common goal or 'wings', flotillas of ships of the same class. For example, the Sixteenth Fleet, assigned to patrol the Federation-Tzenkethi border, contains three wings of three *Akira*-class starships each. Ship groups are usually assembled to complete one task and then disbanded. Occasionally they are commanded by a captain given the temporary position of fleet captain.

In ancient water-based navies where bases of operation were few and far between, admirals literally flew their flag aboard a sailing vessel that was referred to as the fleet's flagship. The tradition of flagships stuck, and Starfleet carried on the tradition. However, the meaning of a flagship has changed over time. Admirals now operate almost exclusively out of starbases, and rarely 'transfer their flag' to a starship. The top-performing vessel within each fleet is honored by their admiral with the title of fleet 'flagship'. One starship in all of Starfleet is considered to be the flagship of the whole fleet, a significant honor and burden that bestows great renown (and possibly infamy) upon one exemplary

EARLIER FLEET OPERATIONS

From the earliest days of Starfleet operations until 2340, Starfleet operated on a task force model rather than as fleets. The reason was simple: Starfleet had too few ships to field one fleet, let alone dozens across known space. During the mid-2260s there were only twelve *Constitution*-class explorers in service, and half of them were lost in action. Starships and their captains operated months away from Federation outposts or stations, and had considerable leeway in determining their best course of action.

Deep-space communication was rudimentary, at best, but gradually got better as Starfleet commissioned more relay satellites and stations throughout Federation space. As the communication network grew, it became easier to coordinate starships. In the meantime, however, it was rare to see two or more starships engaged in the same mission or activity. It took considerable planning to get two starships together to complete a common mission.

It is a testament to the leadership, tenacity, and will of the era's Starfleet officers that the Federation was able to expand during this tumultuous time.

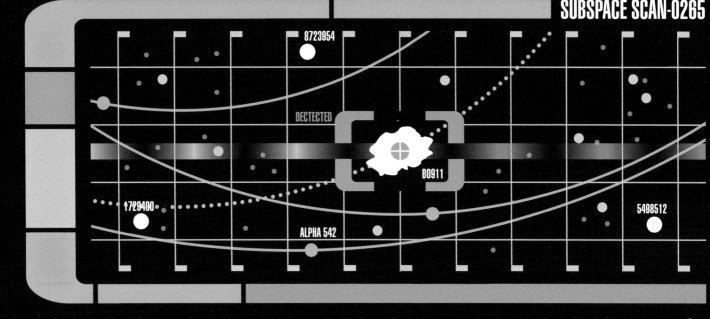

captain and their high-performing crew. The Federation's flagship is currently the *U.S.S. Enterprise*, NCC-1701-D, under Captain Jean-Luc Picard.

A Player's ship will usually be attached to either a standing fleet or a mobile fleet and, while in that fleet, will report to the fleet or sector admiral. Ships within standing fleets may have many of their missions be similar in content, such as patrolling a border or conducting research missions. Mobile fleets are used to resolve specific crises and are thus generally configured with ships that are most useful in a given type of crisis. For example, a tactical mobile fleet may be comprised primarily of heavy cruisers and explorers, while a research mobile fleet may contain light explorers and survey vessels.

There may be times when a ship is assigned to a sector of space for reasons that may not be entirely clear, or a vessel may be tasked to train sensors on particular areas of space at particular times. Such tasks are usually associated with classified mission briefings or priority transmissions from a commanding admiral. Any ship is part of a larger fleet, one that has large-scale responsibilities and duties that may not always appear directly related to a ship's current circumstances, but the chain of command means that captains and crews are operating in the Federation's best interests, not the ship's.

MISSION OPERATIONS

Mission Operations is a Fleet Ops division that focuses on envisioning and creating missions for Starfleet vessels. Part of its planning involves determining the starships and personnel best suited to complete a given mission. Mission Operations receives mission requests from the Federation Council, other Starfleet branches and divisions, and even Federation members, particularly when emergencies arise of a medical or political nature. They take these requests, determine the right mix of ships and crews for the mission, and then forward a brief to Fleet Ops, which disseminates the missions out to the fleet and sector admirals. On rare occasions when time is critical, Mission Operations obtains priority approval from the Fleet Ops Admiralty to deliver a new mission directly to the ship and crew best placed to handle the mission. Such a mission should be treated as if it came from the Federation President himself.

Mission Operations has many analysts, all of whom are experienced logisticians capable of glancing at a mission summary and quickly intuiting what types of starship and officer would be best equipped to handle the task. These analysts are supported by sophisticated computers and databanks that constantly present possible scenarios given a near-endless variety of variables and inputs. Their systems are so sophisticated and reliable that versions are used in Starfleet's Advanced Tactical Division for threat analysis.

Mission Operations also solicits mission concepts and requests from starship captains and sciences officers when the ship and crew make a discovery that warrants more involved exploration or research. In such cases, the request is usually also forwarded to the Research and Exploration branch and jointly coordinated. Both Mission Operations and Research and Exploration have been putting in additional work cycles to develop mission packages for exploring the Gamma Quadrant via Deep Space 9 and the Bajoran wormhole. Despite the new Dominion threat, the wormhole has opened up a vast new territory ripe for exploration.

COMMAND DIVISION
THE JUDICIARY

FEDERATION LAW

This is a quick review of the Federation's government structure, based on the Federation Constitution. There are three major branches: the Executive, which is embodied in the personage of the Federation President; the Legislative branch, consisting of the Federation Council; and the Judiciary, the Federation courts. There are a number of minor branches in the Federation, but this section focuses on the one most likely to be important in the career of a captain: the Judiciary.

THE FEDERATION JUDICIARY

As one of the pillars of the Federation government, it might seem that the Judiciary is too large to be concerned with the actions of a single Starfleet captain. It may also seem that a civilian court system has no jurisdiction in Starfleet matters. Both assumptions are wrong. All captains need to be aware of Federation judicial law and procedures so that if they are faced with a situation that may have Federation-wide implications, they'll know how to proceed legally. When operating on the frontier of the known Galaxy, a starship captain and crew may get involved in legal matters with local governments, and they must have a knowledge of how Federation justice works. They are the representatives of Starfleet and, by extension, the Federation itself. They must behave properly until dedicated Federation judicial officers can be dispatched.

Furthermore, captains are encouraged to study both Federation law and the legalities and procedures of Federation member worlds and protectorates. While the Federation has one body of law and one form of legal procedure, each member world has its own judicial process. Sometimes the two are not entirely harmonious. Being familiar with the diversity of Federation judicial systems is a good preparation for encountering a new species on a new world with a form of government and alien perspective on justice.

JAG OFFICERS

Brief information about two officers who served in the Judge Advocate General's Office.

- **Lieutenant Areel Shaw:** Lt. Shaw was a JAG officer assigned to Starbase 11 in 2267. She prosecuted at the court-martial of Captain James T. Kirk; Kirk was tried for negligence in the death of Lt. Cmdr. Benjamin Finney.

- **Captain Phillipa Louvois:** Captain Louvois has been an active and influential officer within the JAG Corps since the early 2350s. She has been the magistrate on several major cases, including the investigation regarding Lt. Commander Data's sentience in 2365, where she ruled that Data was not the property of Starfleet, and in fact, had the right of free will. Louvois currently commands the Starbase 173 JAG office, located near the Romulan Neutral Zone, and is seen by many as possibly the next Starfleet Judge Advocate General.

STARFLEET JUDGE ADVOCATE GENERAL'S OFFICE

Overseeing all internal legal affairs within Starfleet is the Judge Advocate General's Office, also known as the JAG or the JAG Corps. The Judge Advocate General, currently Rear Admiral Bennett, is a flag officer assigned to Starfleet Command in San Francisco. The JAG has officers at many Federation starbases, and on ally worlds and other key unaligned planets and outposts.

UNIFORM CODE OF STARFLEET JUSTICE (UCSJ)

The Uniform Code of Starfleet Justice (UCSJ) is a system of rules that guides Starfleet's criminal process. Starfleet personnel are tried and may be convicted in a court-martial, or military court, under these rules. The Starfleet court system is completely separate from the civilian Federation Judicial court system. Starfleet has exclusive authority over crimes committed by Starfleet personnel: civilian courts have no say.

For example, a Starfleet court might convene over:

- Failure to obey an order
- Insubordinate conduct
- Mutiny
- Sedition

Most crimes, such as robbery, assault, or murder, violate both civilian and Starfleet law. In such cases the issue becomes whether a Starfleet officer will face a civilian or Starfleet court. Civilian authority is generally based on where the crime was committed; Starfleet authority is based on the status of the offender. If the officer is in active service, the UCSJ applies no matter where the crime occurred. If a crime violates both Starfleet and civilian law, it may be tried by a Starfleet court, a civilian court, or both. The two systems will coordinate to decide how the officer should be prosecuted.

The JAG defends the principles of Starfleet, and this sometimes requires the office to hold hearings against Starfleet officers. It's a form of checks and balances that Starfleet has put into place, with the guidance of the Federation Judiciary branch, to ensure that Starfleet polices its own personnel and makes necessary corrections. Hopefully this is before the higher Federation courts need to be involved, or before a diplomatic incident occurs between the Federation and a non-member world. Starfleet officers take holding themselves accountable very seriously, and the JAG Corps is there to help them all in that respect.

LEGAL PROCEDURES

While considering jurisprudence within the Federation, let's look at three legal areas that play a role in officers' careers, whether they are receiving them or delivering them to a junior: discipline, boards of inquiry, and court-martials.

CREW DISCIPLINE

Any officer aboard a starship or starbase may be disciplined by their department chief, executive officer, or captain (or highest-ranking commanding officer). Some starship standing orders may permit duty watch officers or task leaders to discipline the crew members under their command during a specific duty watch or for a specific assignment. However, it is rare that a department chief of one department will outright reprimand an officer from another department. In most cases, they would discuss the matter with their fellow department chief and then either discipline the officer in question together, or leave it to the officer's own department chief to see to their discipline.

Low-level discipline generally involves a discussion between the officer needing discipline and their commanding officer, either verbally on the spot, or escalated to a written reprimand that is added to an officer's record. More significant reprimands may involve confining the officer to their quarters or in the brig for a period of time (such as 12, 24, or 48 hours), the revoking of certain privileges (reduced or cancelled shore leave, no holodeck access), or mandatory remedial training. In more severe cases, a ship's captain or a starbase commander is authorized to issue a demotion to an officer following a formal board of inquiry, though all such reductions in rank are reviewed by Starfleet Command to ensure procedures and due process were followed. Most of the time the captain's decision is upheld, but in extraordinary cases, the demotion may be overturned, depending on the circumstances and the results of the review.

BOARD OF INQUIRY

When an officer has committed a transgression that a verbal or written reprimand cannot address sufficiently, or when a charge of wrongdoing is placed against them by a Federation citizen, a board of inquiry may be commissioned, a panel of officers from the officer's ship. An officer who feels they have been wrongly disciplined may request a board of inquiry. Such a panel usually consists of the officer's department head, other department heads, the executive officer, and sometimes, the ship's captain.

A board of inquiry is less formal than a court-martial, but is a significant event. If a board of inquiry finds the officer innocent of any wrongdoing, the judgement is noted for the record and the board is dissolved. If the officer is found to have transgressed, the panel will recommend a course of discipline to be carried out by the executive officer or the officer's department head. A board may result in reassignment to another watch, reduction of privileges for a time, or even a demotion. An officer found guilty may appeal to the JAG Corps, in which case a court-martial is convened at the earliest opportunity. An involved Federation or non-Federation citizen who does not agree with the

board's findings may also appeal to the JAG Corps, and again a court-martial is convened as soon as possible. The Diplomatic Corps and the planet's ambassador might also become involved.

COURT-MARTIAL

A court-martial is a formal trial of a Starfleet officer, designed to determine the guilt or innocence of an officer in a specific circumstance. A court-martial has three or more judges, who are always at least Starfleet captains, prosecutors, and one or more defense attorneys unless the officer represents themselves. If an officer is found innocent of any wrong-doing, the verdict is noted in their record and the court is dismissed. If they are found guilty, the court determines the appropriate level of discipline applied, from a formal reprimand added to their record, a demotion in rank or reduction in duties, or even a transfer to a different post. In rare cases, time at a Federation penal facility or even dishonorable discharge from Starfleet may be the proper punishment.

Courts-martial for senior officers are rare, due to Starfleet's effective training programs that begin at the Academy, but also thanks to Starfleet's tendency to look after its own and correct any officer heading down a self-destructive path. Officers are encouraged to interact with their peers professionally and socially, and checking in with a peer group is often a good way to monitor how life in Starfleet is proceeding. This form of cross-department communication is also encouraged because it reinforces the 'one Starfleet' principle. Officers are one fleet with a common purpose, not a collection of disparate departments working their own missions while happening to be aboard the same ship.

PERSONAL LOG EXCERPT

LIEUTENANT SYNOR, JAG OFFICE, STARBASE 109

It has been a month since my transfer from the *U.S.S. Garrett*'s security staff and I find I am settling in to my new role as the junior JAG officer assigned to the station and sector. For the past month, I have struggled to obtain adequate nights of rest. I have attempted to meditate on the matter, and as hard as it is for me to believe the truth of the matter, I believe I am missing the experience of encouraging new discoveries and new worlds with the backdrop of space.

I enjoy my work as a JAG officer though it presents discovery of a different nature. Rather than explore the unknown, I am exploring what is hidden or disguised. Truth has always been a fundamental principle for me, so it seems logical that I would engage in a role

where discovering the truth is of the utmost importance. My senior officer, Commander MacNeill, seems to hold the truth to the same level of respect that I do though sometimes I… wonder. His approach to the investigation and discovery process is lazy, for lack of a better term. Often I find his queries to defendants irreverent and unfocused.

Yet he has somehow achieved acquittals for three such defendants while I have served as his junior, which leads me to suspect that my distraction at transitioning from a shipboard post to a starbase is having a stronger effect on me than I expected. I shall check with Doctor Mul in the morning and see what it has to say about my hypothesis.

COMMAND DIVISION
THE PRIME DIRECTIVE

GENERAL ORDER ONE

The first General Order of Starfleet is also known as the Prime Directive. It is not only a critical piece of Starfleet law but also the guiding philosophy of Starfleet. Every single officer, commissioned and non-commissioned, swears an oath to uphold Federation law and Starfleet regulations, especially the Prime Directive. Defending the Directive may result in the loss of lives, crew, ships, or the oath-takers themselves. The Prime Directive has cost more than a few Starfleet officers their careers.

While the Prime Directive did not formally exist before the 2160s, the general concept of non-interference was a part of Starfleet doctrine from almost the beginning. It has been debated, codified, and refined many times since then, and the current version of it, along with its many exceptions and 47 sub-orders, is a testament to Starfleet's noblest intentions. To date, the Federation is the only political entity with such a non-interference doctrine in place. The Romulans, Cardassians, Klingons, and many other species have very different approaches to handling encounters with less evolved civilizations, some of which might seem a little barbaric in comparison.

Even though the Prime Directive is Starfleet's most important doctrine, it is also challenging to interpret and enforce. Captains interpret the Prime Directive to the very best of their ability and defend their decisions in front of boards of inquiry or courts-martial. The Prime Directive is not treated as an absolute law that must be followed to the letter with no exception every time it might possibly apply. There are as many wrinkles in the Prime Directive's application as there are stars in the Galaxy.

ESSENTIALS

The spirit of the Prime Directive is simply stated, but very hard to enforce and interpret. Basically, it says that Starfleet officers are not to interfere with other civilizations that are unaware of the Federation's existence. Further, if a new culture is not as advanced as the Federation, and specifically does not possess warp-capable vessels, Starfleet is to avoid contact if possible. If exposed to the culture, Starfleet officers should avoid sharing any information about other species, technologies, or knowledge that might influence the development of the encountered culture.

In addition, Starfleet should avoid any action that might affect a civilization's development, such as providing them with an industrial replicator or advanced weaponry. Officers must not involve themselves in another society's affairs, warp-capable or otherwise, until one or more crew members are entangled in some legal or societal issue within the culture.

That is the barest of summaries, and there are lengthy dissertations on the Prime Directive, and captains are expected to be well-versed in them. The bottom line of all arguments is: wherever possible, don't interfere. The real trick for captains is interpreting the Prime Directive in the field, under fire and in a stressful situation. Academy and tactical training cannot compare to real crises in the field.

To illustrate just how difficult the Prime Directive is to interpret and carry out, consider possible responses to the following questions and conundrums. There won't be a test on these later. The purpose is to provoke thinking about the Prime Directive and how interpreting it relates directly to Starfleet's values:

- During a survey of a dying sun, a captain discovers one of the system's planets is inhabited by 100 million people. The culture is a pre-warp capable species, but hidden observation reveals that they are somehow aware of their impending doom. Should they be warned? Should how or why they think their sun will go nova be investigated? What should be done?

- An internal faction of a Federation member world's government reaches out to a captain for assistance, revealing that their new leader is actually a tyrant bent on dismantling the government and pulling the member world out of the Federation. What should be done? Should the faction be assisted, ignored, or reported?

- A starship encounters an alien spacecraft on a direct path for a black hole. They insist Starfleet should not interfere with their societal form of suicide, but one crewman pleads for asylum. What should be done?

Commandant,

My third trade convoy has completed its route and we are returning home to resupply before beginning the next trade cycle. I beg to report that when my ship and crew were enjoying some down-time on the Federation Starbase 212, we were questioned by several Starfleet officers and independent citizens about our cargo, our destination, and our business. We were subjected to what amounted to a cursory inspection of our shipping containers and cargo hold, though I was firm that no one step aboard the ship or look into our personal quarters. While none of my crew was harmed, merely inconvenienced, I have the distinct suspicion that they were concerned that we were Syndicate operatives.

I wish I could say this was the first time this has happened, but it's not. It frustrates me that honest, working citizens of Orion are looked upon with suspicion and concern by non-Orions due to the felonious actions of the Syndicate in Orion's name.

And I know I'm putting myself at risk by even writing this and transmitting it to you. But, I'm struggling to be content with keeping my mouth shut and just conducting business. The Syndicate is a persistent threat to Orion's best intentions. They undermine the work we do, and cast a poor light on the rest of our people. Something has to be done.

While our government has rarely considered Federation application, I sometimes look at Starfleet and the Federation, and their rules and Prime Directive, and I wonder what it would be like to live in such a society, one that actually thinks beyond themselves and considers the impact of their actions and even their non-actions on others. A non-interference policy is a strange concept to many of us, I know, but some nights when I'm watching the stars scroll past my viewport, I wonder what that life must be like, and I want that for my people.

— Captain Bel Hal'aqh

Should the plea be ignored, or should the aliens be convinced not to throw themselves into the black hole?

- A Breen communique is intercepted that indicates the Breen intend to plant an operative on a less-advanced world, then systematically assassinate every key leader so that the Breen can land and enslave the citizens of that world. Should Starfleet confront the Breen, attempt to stop the slavers, notify the primitive culture, defend the world, arm the citizens, or stand idly by?

- A member of a less-advanced world takes one or more Starfleet crew members hostage and demands some form of knowledge or technology in exchange for the prisoners. Failure to deliver will result in the death of one or more of the officers. A second faction on the planet, unaware of the origin of the prisoners, captures them. This second faction makes demands without being aware of Starfleet or the Federation. What does Starfleet do? Attempt a rescue of the crew? Inform the second faction of the truth? Send in disguised security officers to free the prisoners and give them back to the original captors? Mount a hostage rescue? Something else?

APPLICATION

The Prime Directive does not apply equally to all societies on all planets at all times. Although the cornerstone of Federation philosophy, the scope of the Prime Directive varies. It primarily applies to societies that have limited or no knowledge of other worlds or space-faring civilizations, but the Directive also applies to the internal affairs of societies that are aware of other worlds.

There is an application spectrum: the more closely a civilization is tied to the Federation, the more likely it is that interference with that culture will be tolerated to some degree. The Prime Directive will apply to the Klingon Empire, for example, differently than it will to the Bajorans, the Talarians, the Ferengi, the Romulans, the Dominion, or even, theoretically, the Borg. For example, there are still debates whether Captain Picard being the arbiter of succession for the Klingon chancellor was a violation of the Prime Directive. While there were extenuating circumstances involving one of Picard's senior officers, the fact that a Federation officer played a key role in another society's development is something that will be debated for a long time.

A more recent example that is being watched closely by Starfleet Command is Commander Benjamin Sisko's apparent connection to the Bajoran people as some form of prophet or emissary. He has largely resisted this role, though there have been instances where he interacted with the Bajorans in ways beyond what would normally be expected of a Starfleet neighbor. Unsurprisingly, the Prime Directive does not encourage Starfleet officers to present themselves as religious figures within a culture or society.

INTERPRETING THE PRIME DIRECTIVE

Captains are granted enormous leeway when interpreting the Prime Directive in any given mission or circumstance. All Starfleet officers bear responsibility, but the burden falls on a vessel's captain, since they are ultimately responsible for the actions of everyone under their command. No one else on a ship has the authority to interpret the Prime Directive during a mission except the captain, or the executive officer if the captain is unable to command.

In the early years of Starfleet, captains tended to err on the side of intervention, interpreting the Prime Directive as only applying to developing civilizations. Captains might choose to insert their ship and crew into the matter when the civilization had stagnated, became enslaved, or faced immediate danger. Captain James T. Kirk is the most famous (or notorious) officer who represented this classic mode of thinking. His interpretations of the Prime Directive are well-documented, and Starfleet officers still think it wise to review those cases, even though decades have passed and the Galaxy is a very different place.

Some officers have erred on the side of caution and relied more on the letter of the law than its spirit, even when doing so resulted in a significant loss of life or the destruction of entire civilizations. In practice, the Prime Directive applies in specific circumstances and toward certain cultures. It is only peripheral or not relevant at all for other circumstances and other cultures. Plenty of captains have had to wrestle with these concepts, and they were rarely alone in their misery.

Despite Starfleet's need for the Prime Directive to be properly upheld, and the rules involving its interpretation and implementation, captains always have to remember that how they apply will influence their own personal beliefs and values. The Prime Directive is designed to protect Starfleet from getting into moral or legal quagmires it has no business being involved in, but it does not and cannot replace the values which individuals hold dear. Captains are not chosen solely for the ability to follow orders and Federation policies. They have independent thoughts and beliefs, and carry a set of values that have been shaped by life's experiences. When faced with a situation that could involve the Prime Directive, a captain should use their personal beliefs and values as lenses through which to focus both the letter and spirit of the Prime Directive. That way, they can find a solution or ruling to implement without destroying their essential nature.

Everyone in command roles with the possibility of dealing with a Prime Directive issue faces the same concerns, but they are not the first Starfleet captains to wrestle with this issue, and certainly will not be the last. The Directive places significant power in a commander's hands. They must be prepared to accept the consequences of involvement with another culture or species, and face the possibility that involvement causes irreparable harm. The measure of a captain is how that changes their sense of self and conscience.

ASSESSMENT OF THE ALPHA QUADRANT
EXCERPT FROM A DECODED DOMINION REPORT

Of all the powers contained within the Alpha Quadrant, it is the Federation that will require the closest attention. Despite their so-called Prime Directive and the nobility that they tout whenever possible, they are little more than opportunistic expansionists wrapped in a veil of peaceful intentions.

They preach non-interference with less-developed worlds even as they operate secret posts on the very same planets, ostensibly to 'observe' the development of the world's civilization. They refuse to get involved in military and medical crises of peoples who have never encountered them, and in some cases stand by and watch as entire communities die because they 'cannot interfere'. For a people who insist they are compassionate, they certainly allow an unfair share of misery to fall on cultures that the Dominion would have treated with better care, in exchange for their allegiance. A small price to pay, certainly.

The Federation calls themselves an honest people, but the truth is far from reality. They are even worse liars than the Ferengi — and at least with them you know you're being robbed. The Federation offers their utopian society and their industrial replicators and their peaceful intentions, but what they really want is more territory, more starbases, and to be an empire in every way except by name. The Federation orchestrated the alliance with the Klingons and cemented it by maneuvering one of their captains into being the arbiter of succession for Chancellor Gowron. I've even heard rumors that they've sent one of their storied Vulcan ambassadors to Romulus in secret to orchestrate a Vulcan overthrow of the Romulan government under the guide of some sort of re-unification of the two species. Neither of these actions speak well of a people that so vehemently advertises their non-interference.

Should we continue to make advances into the Alpha Quadrant, I expect the Federation will push back as hard as possible, no doubt in an effort to keep their true nature hidden. If they do, we should endeavor to manage events so that they can show themselves as the tyrants they are, even as they refuse to admit it to themselves. Perhaps it's time someone held up a mirror to the precious Federation and forced them to look at the reflection before we send the Jem'Hadar to Earth and show them what it truly means to lead an empire that spans a quadrant.

— Vorta Galeb, Advisor and Assessor

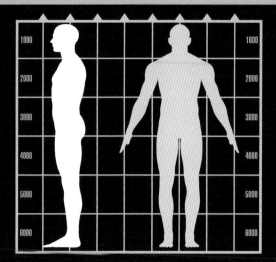

EXCEPTIONS TO THE PRIME DIRECTIVE

There are many recognized exceptions to the Prime Directive, but exceptions do not negate the need for it. When faced with a situation, a captain and crew are mandated to take the least intrusive path, if involvement is warranted or desired. The most common example is when the civilization has been somehow informed, tainted, or contaminated by Starfleet's involvement, intentional or otherwise. Any attempt to reduce or remove the contamination must not, by definition, cause further harm or more interference. Other exemptions include:

- The civilization is already aware of the Federation's existence.

- Members of the civilization communicate with or attack Federation personnel or vessel.

- A universal planetary distress signal is issued.

- The Federation is currently in some form of diplomatic process with the civilization, such as a trade agreement, non-aggression pact, or treaty negotiation.

- The civilization was previously contaminated by Federation citizens or other non-Federation warp-capable species (such as the Ferengi, Cardassians, Klingons, or Romulans).

- Following validated orders from the Federation President, the Federation Council, or the Starfleet Joint Chiefs.

THE TEMPORAL PRIME DIRECTIVE

This related order applies to Starfleet officers who either accidentally or intentionally find themselves time-travelling to the past. It specifically prohibits officers from interfering with past events that could affect the future or the officers' present. This order requires that officers do not give people in the past any information regarding future events. Officers are also prohibited from using advanced technology to solve problems or as conveniences in earlier time frames.

VIOLATING THE PRIME DIRECTIVE

If an officer violates the Prime Directive or the Temporal Prime Directive, willingly or otherwise, they are required to provide detailed notes justifying their reasons. Captains stand alongside any of their officers who have violated the Prime Directive at their board of inquiry or court-martial. Captains also have to provide notes and reasoning as to why their subordinate felt driven to such an act.

The penalties for violating the Prime Directive are nearly as varied as the possible interpretations of the Directive itself, and are usually case specific. In cases where the officer is determined to have acted in the best interests of the civilization in question and the Federation, and potential contamination is eliminated or minimal, nothing may happen other than a symbolic slap on the wrist. In other cases, the officer may be formally reprimanded; transferred to a different position within Starfleet (often a less desirable post); demoted; confined for a period of time in the brig; given extended service time at a Federation penal colony; or dishonorably discharged from Starfleet. In extraordinary cases, life imprisonment may be imposed.

COMMAND DIVISION

STARFLEET ACADEMY AND THE COMMAND DIVISION

DISCOVERING TALENT

As stated earlier, most commanders and captains within Starfleet start in the command division at the Academy. The first year of training and experiences at the Academy have been specifically developed and are constantly updated to enable instructors to determine where officers 'belong' in Starfleet. The Academy is able to predict a cadet's first department with 85% certainty in the first year at the Academy.

Even with that admirable track record, the Academy is not perfect in knowing which cadets will thrive. That's not necessarily the Academy's job. It builds foundations for Starfleet, not career capstones, and cadets are given cross-training across the board, and then trained in specific department tracks based on their performance and experience in the first year. Cadets often switch department tracks in their first and second years at the Academy, less frequently in their third year, and hardly ever in the final year (barring unexpected events). When cadets begin their final year at the Academy, they should have a clear understanding of the role Starfleet has in mind for them as junior-level officers. Conn and command officers are no different.

At any rate, Academy is where it all begins: conn officers are discovered during training and are developed through flight time and training. Command officers are much harder to find, although instructors have made great strides in providing cadets with key training exercises designed to evoke command-type experiences and reactions. Sometimes it's the quiet cadet in the background who shines, rather than the brash cadet hogging the limelight.

A WASTE OF ESPIONAGE

INTERCEPTED OBSIDIAN ORDER COMMUNIQUE

Gul Darale,

I cannot tell you how disappointed I am in Operative Yulis's report from the Starfleet Academy. Given the resources we spent in altering his appearance, embedding him within Starfleet Command, and then helping him break into the Academy training database, the material he returned before he disappeared is pathetic.

Most of his report is material we already knew, but our analysts were most excited by the data packet he provided containing a partial recording of one of Starfleet's key training programs, a scenario revolving around a freighter called the *Koba Mar*, or something to that effect. We anticipated that this scenario would give us insight into how Starfleet trains their officers to the annoying level of competence that our military brethren so often face and struggle to match.

But we found nothing of value. The scenario, as near as our analysts can piece together from the fragmented data, appears to be unwinnable. No cadet is going to have the skill or guile to combat the odds placed against them in the scenario. I suspect this scenario was either a false lead planted by Starfleet to throw off any such infiltration attempt, a suspicion only confirmed by the fact that our operative has not been heard from over the course of three scheduled check-ins. I believe he has been compromised, and with nothing to show for it. Ironic that in his failure to deliver critical intelligence to us, the best he could deliver was a no-win scenario.

— Glinn Tebol, Analyst

COMMAND DEPARTMENT CADETS

Starfleet needs trained, capable captains. It's really as simple as that. Shipyards turn out new starship classes and vessels on a regular basis, and every ship that comes out of spacedock needs a captain on her bridge. There are plenty of qualified officers within the fleet, but the demand for quality captains and commanders never ends. It is for this reason that the Academy places such stock in exercises and training regimens designed to find those rare individuals who show the spark, even within their early days at the Academy, some special quirk that makes them command material.

Command cadets must show a range of skills and abilities, not the least of which is a broad understanding of all the different roles and duties aboard a starship. It doesn't hurt if the candidate knows the difference between an ODN relay and a self-sealing stem bolt, and knows how to repair one and install the other. A captain that can not only order someone to complete a task but who can also do the task on their own when needed will, in all likelihood, inspire their crew. It's human nature to more willingly follow someone who leads by example than by fiat.

Command is not just about having the mental fortitude to send someone to a likely death. Command officers must be able to hold their own in a court of law, across the table in a diplomatic setting, or on the battlefield, whether in the stars or on the ground. A command officer must be a tactician, a diplomat, a negotiator, and a calming influence — sometimes all at the same time. By and large, this is something that cannot be taught. How do you teach someone to be empathetic, or creative? Specific skills, like hostage negotiations or first contact procedures, are learned, but taking on a command position requires something special that sets the command cadets and officers apart.

Furthermore, command cadets must take responsibility for their actions and those under their command, and be ready to accept discipline and punishment for acts they may not have necessarily approved or encouraged. A captain is responsible for the actions of their crew: this has always been the case, and is the reason for having a chain of command. A junior officer is not blameless in the face of a disaster, but the captain in charge will also face at least a board of inquiry, depending on the severity of events. A command cadet must be able to 'take the blame', and be willing and able to defend themselves and their crew.

CONN DEPARTMENT CADETS

Sciences, engineering, medical, and tactical officers all possess skill sets that are expected and somewhat predictable. Even conn officers are relatively easy to pick out: they are the ones with significant flight experience or who demonstrate remarkable skill in flight simulators and training flights. These cadets are usually pegged as conn officers and encouraged to take additional coursework and flight time in order to determine if they have the vision, reflexes, and mathematical prowess to pilot a support craft or starship. Conn officers aren't just pilots: they're expected to be able to understand the deeper math of stellar cartography, astronomy, and astronavigation, and they are expected to be able to calculate warp speeds and travel times in their heads (ship's computers aren't always available). They may not advertise the fact, but conn officers are among the smartest Starfleet officers, which is why some transfer to and from the sciences department.

Conn is an interesting role, one that exemplifies the cross-trained nature of Starfleet. Thanks to modern Starfleet bridge design, every console on the bridge can be reconfigured to the role of any other bridge console. With the touch of a few buttons, a conn officer's helm panel can be the tactical panel or sciences sensor operations panel. The tactical station can become the helmsman's control pad, and so on. In a given extended mission profile, any single conn officer might use their panel for navigation, sensors, tactical events, and managing shipboard operations, without changing station on the bridge. Conn officers may be the best cross-trained officers in the fleet, which is why, statistically, conn officers are the most likely to transfer to a different department after a few years in the service. Across Starfleet there is something of an L-curve of rank at conn: there are a lot of ensigns, junior lieutenants and a few full lieutenants at conn postings, but comparatively fewer lieutenant commanders and hardly any commanders. Conn tends to be a first posting for a junior officer who then learns other positions, transfers to those departments for more training and experience, then transfers back to command to take on an XO position and/or work toward a captaincy.

TESTS OF CHARACTER

Even though it's well over a hundred years old, the old ways are sometimes still good ways. The *Kobayashi Maru* test is one of the classic scenarios the Academy still likes to use on cadets who have been tagged as command candidates. Any cadet can take the test, of course, but it's the command possibles who are most likely to take it. As a pre-designed no-win scenario it's a test of character, much like the range of bridge officer training programs

THE NOVA STARBURST TRANSFER

DECRYPTED MESSAGE FROM THE PRIVATE CADET COMMSERVER

Senior Cadet Vedrak:

Well, here you are. Congratulations. I'll be the first to tell you — you beat the odds. I didn't think we'd see another Tellarite Nova leader for at least another decade. You proved me wrong, and I need you to know how proud I am of you. I enjoyed piloting against you for the last six months in our tactical pilot's course, even though I wasn't confident you had the will and the drive to see it through.

But you did it, and you proved to me and all the flight instructors that there was no contest — there's no other senior cadet with your ability to both pilot the engines off a skimmer and lead a group of pilots to follow you into the same — you are the finest pilot in your class, Cadet, and you should be pleased.

I regret that I cannot hand you the Nova Starburst brooch in person. I was posted to the *Defiant* and we had to make for DS9 like the future of the Federation depended on it. You'll find our squadron's sacred bauble locked securely in the flight commander's office. She'll know the code to open the safe.

Even though I'm not there in person, know that you've earned this honor. I expect you to uphold the honor and heritage of Nova Squadron to the best of your ability, which I know is sterling. Take good care of your team, and be on the lookout for the pilot you'll need to name as Nova leader after you. Our tradition is long, and Nova Squadron will endure. Peace and clear skies to you, my friend.

— Ensign Lavar Blackmon, *U.S.S. Defiant*

available to any officers aboard starships interested in adding bridge duties to their repertoire of skills. These scenarios are designed to force test subject to evaluate a difficult decision and make hard choices that may result in the deaths of fellow officers or friends. Most species have the preservation of others hard-wired into their ethics, so the Academy plays on that to determine if a command candidate understands that it can be necessary to sacrifice one for the good of the all. Captains will face situations where they hold the power of life and death in their hands, based on the orders they give.

COMMAND DIVISION
STARSHIP OPERATIONS AND COMMAND OFFICERS

STARSHIP HIERARCHY

Starfleet's overall chain of command was discussed earlier, but on a starship the chain of command always ends at the captain. The captain is the highest level of authority aboard and, barring extraordinary circumstances, a captain's orders cannot be countermanded except by an officer above them in station or rank. To use an ancient Earth phrase, the buck stops here.

Those extraordinary circumstances will be covered shortly, but for now let's discuss the differences between general orders, orders, and regulations. All three are part and parcel of serving in Starfleet, and a command-level officer must understand them completely.

GENERAL ORDERS

Starfleet's general orders are directives and guidelines that provide structure and direction to Starfleet personnel in carrying out all missions of exploration and defense. They are the foundations upon which Starfleet stands, and they provide guidance on all manner of topics from first contact protocols to recommended starbase etiquette and the proper compilation and distribution of scientific surveys. The Prime Directive, discussed earlier, is the most important and most well-known outside of Starfleet, but officers must be knowledgeable about all of them. This is no small task given that there are well over a hundred general orders.

While the list of General Orders may seem extensive (and even exhaustive) they exist to help when faced with mission situations on assignment. They are there to guide as much as they are there to protect. While the Alpha Quadrant may feel a little smaller than it did back in the 23rd century — when

OTHER GENERAL ORDERS AND DIRECTIVES

Aside from the Prime Directive, there are other general orders. These include:

- **General Order 7:** Prohibits any form of contact with the planet Talos IV.

- **General Order 12:** Requires a captain and/or crew to take appropriate precautions when approached by a starship with which communications have not been, or cannot be, established.

- **General Order 15:** Involves procedures revolving around the safety of flag officers, including a requirement that an armed escort must be provided when beaming into hazardous or potentially hazardous situations.

- **Order 104, Section C:** This regulation details the procedures the chief medical officer must undertake to relieve a commander of their duty. The physician is required to document their proof that the commander is mentally or physically unfit or somehow rendered incapable of command. A detailed physical and mental examination of the commander is also required.

- **Directive 010:** Establishes the protocol that before engaging a species in battle, Starfleet personnel must attempt to make first contact with them and attempt to find a non-violent solution.

- **Directive 101:** Affords the right of silence to all Starfleet officers facing a board of inquiry or court-martial.

a Federation starship could be months away from the nearest starbase — captains often find themselves out of easy reach of a starbase or a flag officer. When that occurs, or when faced with a time-sensitive situation, captains rely on their understanding of general orders and interpret them as best they can.

There have been numerous occasions when Starfleet captains and officers have adjusted, ignored, or violated the spirit of the General Orders to serve a purpose. Invariably, you will find yourself faced with a situation with no easy answer and no black-and-white solution coupled to an easily-quotable General Order subsection. Sometimes you just have to use the General Orders as inspiration for your solution and be prepared to justify your reasoning at the follow-up board of inquiry. Violations of General Orders have resulted in disciplinary actions, including boards of inquiry, courts-martial, reprimands, demotions, and in some cases, periods of detention at a Federation penal facility.

STANDING ORDERS

Orders or 'standing orders' are the expectations or requirements a captain develops as part of their command philosophy and imparts to a crew. Standing orders may change depending on the needs of the captain or crew, or may be dropped if a crisis passes or thanks to changing circumstances. While directives and general orders rarely change, standing orders may change regularly, but particularly when a ship changes commander. A captain tends to carry standing orders from posting to posting, the list growing and changing as the captain learns from experience and picks the orders that work best with their command style to fulfill missions from Mission Operations and Starfleet Command.

It's not possible to provide a complete list of standing orders, but these few are common to many captains and admirals. Captains should be encouraged to come up with their own orders, and to create more as needed:

- The captain shall be announced when seen coming on the bridge ("Captain on the bridge").

- During mission briefings, all officers shall remain standing unless expressly invited to sit by the officer conducting the briefing.

- The ship shall maintain a rotation of four duty watches, designated Alpha, Beta, Gamma, and Delta.

- A Level 3 diagnostic shall be conducted on all shipboard systems during every Gamma watch. The results will be provided to the executive officer, who give a summary to the captain by 0500 every day.

- The bridge shall be fully staffed during all duty watches.

DIRECTIVES

Directives, in *Star Trek Adventures*, provide the whole Player group a core belief, statute, or order to follow for their mission. Directives are a Value that can be accessed by the whole group, and cited in order to use Determination.

Directives can take the form of any general orders, orders, or regulations the crew might be under but they only apply to one mission. The Gamemaster should make known any Directives in play at the beginning of the mission, and repeat that at the beginning of each game session until the mission is complete. The Prime Directive is always considered to be in play, and can be quoted for the use of Determination by any Starfleet character.

EXAMPLE DIRECTIVES:

- Resolve the negotiations peacefully.
- Defend the colonists by any means necessary.
- Do not transmit messages 'in the clear'. All messages must be coded.

REGULATIONS

Starfleet regulations are the procedures and codes of conduct that form the common basis of service for all Starfleet personnel. Details such as standard procedures for alert status, shipwide systems diagnostics, maintenance procedures, handling promotions and transfers, and other details of life in Starfleet are covered in regulations or procedures. Most Starfleet regulations are the same throughout the fleet: for example, the regulation for the proper calibration of a shuttle's port sensor array is always the same wherever a shuttle is found. Starship and starbase commanders are required to post individual amendments to regulations for crew to access easily. Much of the time changes a commander makes to regulations are often reflected in their standing orders.

STARSHIP OPERATIONS

There are many regulations revolving around the standard operation of a Starfleet vessel. There isn't space to go into all of them, so these are the most critical, and the ones most likely to be important to operations.

ALERT STATUS

A starship or starbase normally operates under one specific status at a time. The various types of operational status are referred to as an alert status or an operational mode:

Cruise Mode: A standard peacetime operating procedure. The crew are free to perform regular duties during the watch rotation. Partial weapon systems are on a two-minute readiness level, one shuttle is at launch readiness, and level-4 diagnostics are run on all key systems at the start of each watch, unless otherwise dictated by a standing order.

Yellow Alert: A mode of increased crew awareness. Yellow alert status can be invoked by the watch officer, operations manager, chief engineer, tactical officer, or the leader of the ship's current mission activity. Level-4 diagnostics are immediately performed on all key systems and subsystems; warp and impulse engines are brought to full operational power if not there already; defensive systems and weapons are brought to increased readiness. All senior staff members are notified of the status and backup watch personnel are expected to be ready to serve.

Red Alert: Invoked during emergencies, combat situations, or whenever the ship or crew are in immediate peril. All duty shift personnel are notified and are expected to be prepared for action. All senior staff members are required to report to their duty stations. Level-3 diagnostics are immediately performed on critical systems (engines, warp power, weapons), and level-4 diagnostics are run on all other systems. Low-priority systems (such as science experiments and holodecks) are put on standby or shut down. Weapons and defensive systems are brought to full readiness and shields are immediately raised. Only the captain, executive officer, and watch officer can invoke Red Alert.

Intruder Alert: This mode is for any known or perceived internal security matter. Nonessential personnel are confined to their current locations, and there is authorized access only to all turbolifts and sensitive ship stations. Security officers are assigned to key ship locations such as the bridge and main engineering. Deck-by-deck physical and automated security sweeps attempt to locate the intruder(s).

Medical Alert: If there is a biological outbreak aboard, this mode requires all personnel to be confined to their current location until medical personnel isolate and resolve the crisis. This reduces the likelihood of any contagion or outbreak spreading through the ship. The commanding officer and the chief medical officer may declare a medical alert.

DUTY WATCHES

Starfleet standard procedures recommend a three 8-hour watch rotation aboard starships and starbases, with the first watch starting at 0001 hours and ending at 0800, the second running 0801 to 1600 hours, and the third watch from 1601 to 0000 hours (midnight). Captains and starbase commanders often alter the timing of duty watches. Some extend the start and end of the shifts by 5-15 minutes to allow a status briefing for the incoming watch staff. Captains are largely allowed to decide when shifts begin and end, and issue changes to the crew as a standing order.

Some captains choose a four-watch rotation. There are pros and cons in this, but it can be useful to switch watch patterns to keep a crew sharp and ready to adjust to change. A four-watch rotation has four 6-hour periods, which gives more flexibility to crew members, allows time for additional study and duty, and helps to reduce fatigue since officers are standing shorter watches. However, a four-watch pattern requires enough experienced officers within each department to lead each watch and, for smaller ships and outposts, this may mean one officer ends up standing two watches in one day, increasing rather than reducing fatigue.

SHIP DIAGNOSTICS

The major systems and subsystems in use aboard Starfleet vessels and stations have a series of diagnostic tools built into them for use during standard operations or during an alert status. These tools are designated in levels, with each level requiring a different level of automation instead of crew member involvement. The type of diagnostic used depends on the situation and time available. Captains may be put in a position where they need to request one or more levels of diagnostic on the ship's systems:

Level 1: The most comprehensive diagnostic, Level 1 involves a team of officers working together to verify automated system diagnostics and mechanisms in cases where the results coming from the automated systems

AN OFFICER'S DAY

COMMANDER ROBERT DELACOURT'S THREE-WATCH ROTATION

0600 End sleep period
0630 Exercise regimen
0730 Breakfast with Lieutenant DeVries and her subordinates; discuss ongoing science experiments
0815 Watch transfer
0830 Begin day watch
1230 Lunch break with Chief Engineer Jenson
1615 Watch transfer
1630 End day watch
1700 Violin lessons
1745 Cadet orientation to turbolift control
1830 Dinner with middle grade debate team champions
1945 Personal time
2200 Begin sleep period

cannot be trusted. A Level 1 diagnostic usually requires the system and subsystems being diagnosed to be taken off-line, and may take several hours to complete.

- **Level 2:** This is similar to a Level 1 in that it also requires some crew member verification of a suite of automated scans, but is less comprehensive and a little less reliable. A Level 2 diagnostic takes approximately half the time of a Level 1 diagnostic.

- **Level 3:** This step is similar to Level 1 and 2, but requires only key systems and automated results to be verified by a crew member. Standard operation procedure sets a benchmark of 10 minutes to begin and complete a Level 3 diagnostic.

- **Level 4:** This is an automated procedure initiated by a crew member or by the ship's computer under certain operational modes or alert status levels. When a problem within a system is suspected, a Level 4 diagnostic is run and completed within 30 seconds in most cases.

- **Level 5:** Like Level 4, this is an automated procedure that is intended for routine use on all major ship systems, especially those that see regular use on day-to-day basis. Level 5 diagnostics are generally completed within 2 seconds. Some operational modes and alert status levels trigger immediate Level 5 diagnostics, and many captains create standing orders requiring regular Level 5 diagnostics on all key ship systems.

CHAPTER 02.80

COMMAND DIVISION
YOUR SENIOR STAFF

YOUR SUPPORT STRUCTURE

The captain is the leader aboard their starship. Supporting the captain is a group of other leaders: some are inherited with the ship, and some are hand-picked from a small pool of candidates. These senior-level officers, sometimes referred to as the senior staff and sometimes as the ship's C-level officers (C-level because they're all 'chiefs' — chief engineer, chief medical officer, chief of security, etc.), are the leaders of their departments aboard the ship. They are there to support the captain's orders, manage their staff, and provide experience and skill to inform the captain's decisions. The senior staff will invariably comprise a diverse selection of individuals. It's a foolish captain who doesn't listen to their counsel, because the group working together is going to make better decisions than one person standing alone.

The chain of command is not a democracy. It's rare that any decision will come to a vote by the senior staff. Starfleet does not make captains to be the chair of a ruling council. The captain is there thanks to showing the ability to make a choice from a selection of hard choices, informed by their own experiences and the advice, counsel, and experiences

of the senior staff and crew. The officers serving aboard a starship can make suggestions and give a captain the best insights and data possible but, ultimately, the decision is made alone.

It's now time to consider the most important of the senior staff, the single most important officer aboard a ship after the captain: the executive officer.

THE EXECUTIVE OFFICER

The executive officer, XO, first officer, "Number One" — or any number of other terms and nicknames — is the captain's most important asset and ally. While the captain has to manage the overall direction of the ship and crew, and wrestle with the big issues such as how interpret Starfleet's orders, the executive officer's duty is to see that ship and crew function at the peak of their abilities. Maintenance and personnel issues, personnel reviews, and discipline are just a few of the tasks carried out by the XO. The XO normally leads all away team missions and, even if they're not the leader, they have a key role in assigning away team officers, placing the captain's safety first in all circumstances. A ship without its captain cannot function adequately, and so an XO looks to the captain's safety first, the crew second, and the ship third.

The XO is a captain's most important officer, and they need to be carefully selected for the role. It's rare for Starfleet to dictate a choice of XO to a captain, but Starfleet Command or a sector admiral might make suggestions or advise about appropriate XOs. In the end, it's the captain's choice. Depending on the class and size of a vessel, a captain may have a full commander as XO. Smaller ship classes usually have a lieutenant commander as XO instead. While it's not standard practice or as common as it used to be, the XO can also be a department head aboard ship. For example, Lieutenant Commander Spock served aboard Kirk's Enterprise as both executive officer and sciences chief. The

workload for one officer as both an XO and department head role is significant, but certainly achievable with the right candidate.

Captains, choose an XO with care. Not only will they be supporting and sometimes even challenging the person in the center chair but, to be morbid for a moment, the XO may be required to replace the captain at some point.

OTHER SENIOR STAFF MEMBERS

After appointing an XO, a captain works with them to develop the duty roster and hierarchy of command aboard their ship. While the hierarchy is generally laid out through standard Starfleet regulations and general orders, a captain has some flexibility in who they choose for roles aboard the ship.

THE SECOND OFFICER

Captains also need to appoint a second officer who, despite the name, is the third in command of the vessel after the captain and the XO, and may be the department head of a non-command department such as engineering or sciences. Captains are encouraged to pick the most qualified and experienced officer as a second, but many like to use the second officer role as training for up-and-coming officers. In addition to regular duties, Seconds tend to stand third watch in the standard rotation, and this gives them valuable command experience on the bridge during a time when there

THE XO ROLE PLUS ONE

If your campaign is set on a small ship or if you have a small number of Players, you may choose to have a Player Character perform both the Executive Officer role and one other role such as XO/Chief of Sciences or XO/Chief of Security. Any Player Character taking on two Roles must choose one of the two role benefits for their character (as detailed on pages 126-127 of the core rulebook) but may not use both benefits.

BEING THE BEST CAPTAIN YOU CAN BE

You are a starship captain. As such, you are the commander of your vessel and leader of your crew. You are responsible for the lives and actions of everyone aboard, Starfleet and civilian alike. Should anyone under your command commit a crime or violate Federation law (or the law of a non-Federation world), you will be held responsible. Yours is a challenging role, and you must take care that responsibility does not turn into a burden too difficult to bear.

The very best Starfleet captains lead by example. Not only have they attempted the tasks that they ask of their officers, but they will actively engage in 'time-filler' tasks to show that they are willing to do anything they order a subordinate to do. Some captains engage with their crews by creating a collegial atmosphere, while others prefer to maintain a stricter level of decorum and a separation between themselves and the crew. Most captains insist upon an 'open door' policy to their ready room, though for some this is more lip service than reality.

As captain, you will determine your own style of command and find what works for you in eliciting the very best results from your ship and crew. Starfleet does not issue easy orders to its starships and captains: you will rarely get a 'milk run' mission. Starfleet's work, under the leadership of its captains, is profoundly challenging and mission success rests squarely upon your shoulders.

Spend time getting to know your crew and ship. Be willing to explore every Jefferies tube and conduit of your vessel. Learn every deckplate groan or ODN relay click. Interview all the officers under your command, including the non-coms and the civilians aboard, whether they are Starfleet families or Federation civil servants. Take advanced classes when you can, attend seminars, and cultivate some hobbies you can embrace when you are not fully focused on command. Be willing to consult your senior staff for mission input, and rely on your ship's doctor or chief counsellor for confidential advice on whatever matters weigh on you.

are no scheduled mission activities. While challenges and disasters do not obey the clock, third shift is a good place to develop younger officers.

CHAIN OF COMMAND

Once a second is selected, captains consider it good practice to follow standard Starfleet regulations for the ship's chain of command, though sometimes the chain is adjusted depending on personal preferences and mission parameters. Captains with a significant background in security, tactical, or engineering may select the wearer of a gold uniform over red or blue out of respect and loyalty, but this is tempered by practicality. A veteran engineering head is likely to be a more effective leader than a journeyman lieutenant out of security, no matter how much the captain appreciates the 'brotherhood' of tacticians.

Just as the ship's chain of command is selected by the captain with help from the XO, department chains of command and hierarchies are established by senior staff department heads who may ask for guidance. Usually it is the XO who aids the department heads in determining effective personnel allocations. The XO and department heads will work together to staff every department and position on the ship so that the ship has experienced leaders and crew on hand during all watches.

DEVELOPING YOUR OFFICERS

In addition to their other duties, captains are expected and required to see to the professional development of the officers under their command. While captains do not necessarily monitor and evaluate crew on a day-to-day basis like the XO, they are expected to offer ample opportunities to everyone aboard that are designed to help them grow in their Starfleet career. They are also encouraged to help them develop as individuals, but the primary task for captains is to contribute to the development of officers.

Why? The answer is simple: Starfleet is a continually growing and changing organization. Every month, new starships leave Federation spacedocks, crew members transfer, retire, make the ultimate sacrifice, or are lost to a myriad of phenomena that are part of the reality of exploring the cosmos. While personnel turnover within Starfleet is acceptable, there is turnover and a constant need for officers at all levels, particularly capable officers who can serve as captains and XOs.

Beyond that, Starfleet has an ongoing need for shrewd and talented flag-level officers. Every admiral has worked their way up through the ranks over decades of service, and every new starbase, extended frontier, or new subdivision

of Starfleet Command, needs admirals. Existing admirals take extended leave or eventually retire, and their posts must be filled with experienced and qualified senior officers. There is a long-term career for any Starfleet officer with the talent and ambition to keep moving forward and learning. Captains are expected to help fellow officers along the path when possible.

TRANSFERS TO THE COMMAND DIVISION

Captains, their XOs, and department heads are encouraged to remind all officers aboard that the three Starfleet divisions are not gated silos with difficult entrance exams. There is significant flexibility within Starfleet for an officer to transfer between departments and divisions with a minimum of headache and procedures. As long as officers meet the position requirements, current department service is significantly less important than the skills and experience they can bring to a new posting and whether they can perform with a high level of competence.

Officers have transferred from conn to engineering, from security to sciences, and every other combination of department and division imaginable. Since the Federation encourages growth and personal development in all its citizens, Starfleet officers are likewise encouraged to expand their skillsets and to cross-train to the best of their abilities.

To foster this dedication to learning and cross-training to your crew, captains should practice what they preach and engage in tasks that aren't normal 'captain-type' tasks. Captains can host training seminars on a wide range of topics and encourage qualified officers to do the same. Friendly competitions between different departments or different duty watches are also encouraged. Captains should expect officers to come up with creative solutions to strange problems. Watch rosters should rotate, and captains occasionally surprise duty officers with spot appearances or scenarios designed to test their ability to operate as a cross-functional team. Officers that show the most effective flexibility are the ones captains want to monitor for possible promotions or transfer to other departments.

PERSONAL LOG EXCERPT

LIEUTENANT SAKETH, U.S.S. EAGLE

I have to admit that today was one of the more perplexing days I've experienced under the command of Captain MacDougall, and within my Starfleet career to date.

I engaged in, and completed, the bridge officer training today, and while my close friend, Yeoman Bailey, is confident that the captain and XO feel I passed the test successfully, I believe I must have failed the effort based on the reactions of my fellow officers during the course of the test.

During the test, while engaged in what seemed to be a routine recalibration of the port sensor array, a Romulan warbird decloaked off our port bow and the *Eagle* was soon under fire. I maintained my post in main engineering, though I shifted my task efforts from the sensor recalibration to my red alert stations, as per protocol.

During the battle, the ship suffered structural damage to the starboard warp nacelle which damaged a number of power transfer conduits between main engineering and the warp nacelle. The damage was significant enough that a small repair team, or perhaps one skilled officer, would need to be sent into the Jefferies tubes to effect repairs.

As Chief Engineer Pearson was on the bridge and otherwise engaged with duties, it fell to me to make the decision as to who to send. Considering the variables involved and the skill levels of the

crew available to me, I ordered Lieutenant Heyden to take a repair kit and a sealer and go repair the damage. I estimated his probability of success at 97 percent, though I also estimated his probability of surviving the radiation poisoning at less than 12 percent.

I wisely chose not to share these percentages with him, however. I have discovered that some species do not like to be reminded of their own mortality. Regardless, he was the most logical choice and I ordered him to make repairs immediately.

To his credit, he completed the repairs as expected. Also as expected, he died following the repair effort. The loss of his expertise, had this been a real crisis, would have been keenly felt within engineering and throughout the ship.

After sharing these thoughts with my messmates I was treated to blank stares and disappointed looks. I inquired of Lieutenant Baker about these unexpected reactions, and she muttered something about my lack of empathy.

I have yet to determine what role empathy has to play in making a life or death command decision. Perhaps after I receive the results of my examination, I will ask the XO for her opinion.

COMMAND DIVISION CHARACTERS

28340772291024
13350048399

COMMAND DIVISION CHARACTERS
COMMAND SCHOOL

"PART OF BEING A CAPTAIN IS KNOWING WHEN TO SMILE. MAKE THE TROOPS HAPPY! EVEN WHEN IT'S THE LAST THING IN THE WORLD YOU WANT TO DO. BECAUSE THEY'RE YOUR TROOPS, AND YOU HAVE TO TAKE CARE OF THEM."

— BENJAMIN SISKO

THE BURDENS OF COMMAND

Command is an inseparable mix of privilege and responsibility. Officers who take on command duties have considerable leeway in their actions, decisions, and the methods by which they carry out missions. Freedom is balanced by a duty to serve as a proper representative of Starfleet and the United Federation of Planets and by duty to their ships and crews. It is not a light burden, or an easily given privilege.

Characters with a high Command Discipline are familiar with this dichotomy, and many will have learned about it from the lessons of the past. They have studied the missions of Archer and Kirk (among others) to understand the burdens and challenges of starship command.

Command is not purely leadership: the spirit and composure of the role is valuable for all Starfleet officers, from a security officer coordinating tactics to a medical officer advising a patient. Command is valuable for characters seeking to persuade or convince, and for those trying to resist coercion. Command officers know that command of self leads to command of others.

FLAG RANKS

The highest rank available to Player Characters is captain, but there is the potential for veteran commanding officers of starships to grow and develop. Some captains regard this idea with dismay: they joined Starfleet to explore, push frontiers, and command starships, not sit in Starfleet Headquarters, and they view the Admiralty as tantamount to retirement.

This is not entirely accurate. Many admirals have moved on from front-line command duties, and they deal with the Machiavellian twists of fleet policy. For some groups, playing out the exploits of an admiral and their supporting staff is just as compelling as commanding a starship deep in the unknown.

THE ADMIRALTY

An Admiralty campaign has differences to a typical campaign as described in the *Star Trek Adventures* core rulebook. The most obvious of these is that the commanding officer isn't a captain, but a flag officer with different responsibilities.

It is unusual for any two flag officers to have identical responsibilities. During times of peace, an admiral is likely to oversee operations in a given region, the actions of a specific group of ships (a squadron, wing, or fleet, depending on ship numbers), or run a specific set of related activities. For example, Vice Admiral (later Fleet Admiral) Alynna Nechayev oversaw operations along the Federation/Cardassian border in the 2360s and early 2370s. Responsibilities change over time, and admirals are redeployed to different regions, groups, or portfolios every few years, overseen by Starfleet's chiefs of staff. The chiefs have to consider the bigger picture of the Federation and its neighbors, and their decisions could impact trillions of lives.

RANKS IN THE ADMIRALTY

There are four distinct ranks within the Admiralty, which are described below. The proper form of address for all of these ranks is "admiral".

- **Rear Admiral:** A term from British naval tradition. A large fleet would be commanded by three admirals: the senior overseeing everything from the center, a second with the leading ships, and the most junior at the back of the fleet. This organization is centuries out of date, but the names remain. Rear admirals are the junior admirals in Starfleet. By the 24th century, the rank is divided into rear admiral, lower half and rear admiral, upper half.

- **Vice-Admiral:** These flag officers typically command large numbers of starships, or oversee many sectors. A vice-admiral must sometimes command operations in an entire theatre — a region bordering another power, such as the Romulan Neutral Zone or the Cardassian Demilitarized Zone, especially when there is turmoil or unknown peril. For vice-admirals and above rank tends to matter less than individual experience and expertise: Starfleet may assign a vice-admiral, admiral, or even a fleet admiral to a particular command depending on who is available and the prevailing situation.

- **Admiral:** Admirals have greater authority and responsibility than vice-admirals, though in practice they are deployed in a similar manner. A large number of admirals serve primarily as administrators.

- **Fleet Admiral:** Fleet admirals are at top of the chain of command. They have the greatest responsibilities and the greatest authority. Fleet admirals are most likely to serve as administrators in Starfleet Command, and few are active in the field.

ADMIRALTY MISSIONS

Command of a group of vessels, or all Starfleet activities in a particular region of space, has a lot of flexibility for a flag officer, and it also defines the nature of an Admiralty campaign. There is a considerable overlap between the missions below, though the lines between them can be vague. They are a useful start when considering the roles and responsibilities of admirals:

- **Group Command:** The admiral commands several vessels. These have their own captains, but the admiral determines the missions undertaken. When vessels of similar or complimentary types perform missions together, the admiral selects one as the flagship, and oversees from that ship's bridge or other command center. Alternatively, different vessels may perform individual, related missions, and the Admiral will work from a nearby starbase, or move their flag to whichever vessel demands closer oversight at that time. The group may work in a particular location, deployed as a single unit to deal with a particular problem, explore a particular area, or support a specific set of activities.

- **Theatre Command:** The admiral commands Starfleet operations in a particular region of space, and treats with allies and neutral parties within the region. There will be a number of starships that the Admiral can use, but additional support can be requested for a particular operational need. Starfleet has numerous vessels that largely operate independently, responding when an admiral requests support. Admirals on theatre command duties will operate from a major starbase. Some take direct command of the starbase; others

leave its running to a dedicated crew. And admiral can always move flag to a vessel if the situation needs close oversight.

- **Operation Command:** The admiral is responsible for military, diplomatic, exploratory, scientific, technical or intelligence missions, and can call on individual vessels and personnel when required. These admirals are proven experts and will normally only command a single vessel or small squadron, but will move ships as the situation dictates. An unusual type of command as few admirals have the Starfleet-renowned specific expertise desirable this role.

PLAYING ADMIRALTY CAMPAIGNS

Admiralty campaigns produce an experience that is distinct from starship or starbase campaigns. Admirals look at the broader implications of events, beyond just their own responsibilities to ship, crew, and duty, and are placed in demanding situations where there are no easy answers.

An Admiralty game focuses rather more on the politics of the Galaxy than a traditional game does. This is ideal fodder for some Players, but uninteresting to others. While Starfleet officers should be diplomatic, admirals are often the ones dealing with the repercussions of those officers' decisions.

BETWEEN CAPTAIN AND ADMIRAL

Two ranks exist between captain, commonly regarded as the senior line rank, and admiral, thanks to tradition and administrative needs:

COMMODORE

In the 22nd and 23rd centuries, the rank of commodore existed as an intermediate step between captain and admiral. Officers were officially part of Starfleet Command, and each was responsible for several vessels, rather than one, but their duties were in the field rather than at the Admiralty. By the early 24th century commodores had been phased out, and suitable officers were promoted to the rank of rear admiral, lower half.

FLEET CAPTAIN

In some cases, captains assigned as adjutants or chiefs of staff to an admiral receive a promotion to the rank of fleet captain. Christopher Pike received this honor after his time in command of the *Enterprise*, and Garth of Izar was a fleet captain before his descent into madness. This rank acknowledges an officer's increased responsibilities and, on a practical level, clears them for information and intelligence which line officers are not normally permitted to see.

The specific form an Admiralty game takes depends on where and when it is set: a game on the 24th Century Cardassian border may find Players embroiled in tense international politics and even warfare; peace and trade connections may dominate a game on the Klingon border after the Khitomer Accords. Even so, there are common elements.

THE CHARACTERS

The Admiralty campaign is focused on the admiral, like a starship or starbase campaign is built around the captain. The admiral doesn't need to be a Player Character; the Gamemaster could run a Non-Player Character with the action and decision-making focused on the Main Characters as the admiral's staff.

Regardless of how the admiral is played, the remaining Main Characters will be the admiral's staff, personnel from the admiral's flagship or base, as well as personnel from vessels, facilities, and groups under the admiral's command. This may give a group of Main Characters that is not interconnected because duties and responsibilities are spread over several ships.

To alleviate this, an admiral's campaign will normally have access to more Crew Support than a single vessel would, as will be covered later.

Characters may select any of the following roles, in addition to those described in the core rulebook. Normal roles may

be selected multiple times if characters duplicate roles are assigned to different vessels or starbases. The group could contain multiple commanding officers so long as each commands a different group (normal role abilities apply only to the character's own ship and crew). When a Supporting Character is introduced they may be assigned to any role vacant on their vessel or starbase, so you could have a Supporting Character serve as chief engineer on any of the ships under the admiral.

- **Admiral:** Flag officer only. In an Admiralty game, the group must have an admiral (even if they're a Non-Player Character). *Select three additional Focuses, reflecting areas of expertise or subjects that pertain to the admiral's assignment. At the start of each mission, the admiral chooses one of their three Focuses, and every Main Character receives that as an additional Focus for the mission, due to additional briefings and instructional resources.*

- **Adjutant:** Command department only. The adjutant must be at least a lieutenant commander. This is the admiral's closest advisor and assistant, providing aid and support like an executive officer supports a commanding officer. A good adjutant is always prepared with mission proposals, alternative plans, and hypothetical scenarios to allow the admiral to react to problems. *At the start of any scene, the adjutant may spend one Momentum (Immediate) in order to change the Focus chosen by* *the admiral for the duration of that scene only. The new Focus must be one of the others selected by the admiral.*

- **Strategic Operations Officer:** Command department only. This officer coordinates the movements and activities of vessels and forces in a given region or on a particular mission. Typically officers with a keen understanding of strategy, they advise the admiral and adjust plans independently when they cannot consult the admiral. *Regardless of rank, the strategic operations officer has authority over all vessels and forces linked to their region or mission. They may reduce the Difficulty of Persuade Tasks with the commanding officers of those vessels and forces by 1, to a minimum of 0.*

- **Intelligence Officer:** An intelligence officer receives Starfleet Intelligence, other branch and Federation ally reports on strategic and diplomatic developments in the region. These reports, and analyses, allow the officer to inform the admiral and other cleared personnel about matters that might impact decisions. *Once per mission, an intelligence officer may create an Advantage without requiring a Task or spending any resources. This Advantage reflects some detail or insight the officer learned in an intelligence report.*

- **Fleet Liaison Officer:** A fleet liaison represents the interests of the fleet, and Starfleet as a whole, to one of the Federation's allies. A Starfleet officer will represent the Federation, though the Gamemaster may allow other fleet liaison officers; for example, a joint Klingon-Federation task force may include a Klingon Empire liaison. These officers report to superiors and allow cooperation between allies. *The fleet liaison officer has an additional Trait: **Contacts Amongst X**, where X is the fleet or service the liaison works with/for. For example, a Klingon Defence Force has the trait **Contacts Amongst the Klingon Defence Force**.*

- **Diplomatic Attaché:** A civilian from the Federation Diplomatic Corps and a valuable part of the staff who advises the admiral, and briefs them on culture, protocol, and other essential information during negotiations and other diplomatic activities. *At the start of any Social Conflict involving a foreign culture, the diplomatic attaché may spend two Momentum (Immediate) to create an Advantage for any Main Character present, representing a briefing provided by the attaché. This may be performed even if the attaché character is not personally present in that scene; it is prior counsel, rather than immediate assistance.*

THE SQUADRON

When an admiral commands several ships, changes need to be made for an Admiralty campaign. Instead of a single starship, the admiral should be provided with several ships,

ROLES IN OTHER GAMES

With the exception of admiral and adjutant, many of these new roles could be used in a game focused on a single ship or starbase. Indeed, Lieutenant Commander Worf serves as strategic operations officer, fleet liaison to the Klingons, and intelligence officer on Deep Space 9. In game terms, he would only benefit from one role, even though he performs all three. Similarly, Major Kira Nerys is a liaison from the Bajoran Militia to Starfleet.

While uncommon, it is possible for characters to use flag ranks in an otherwise ordinary game structure. In these situations, the Admiral takes the Commanding Officer role, and any Command character with a rank of Captain or below may be executive officer. Although unorthodox, this can happen in situations where an experienced crew serves together for a protracted period, with senior staff who are all high rank: an example is Rear Admiral Kirk taking command of the *U.S.S. Enterprise* during the first three *Star Trek* movies.

which can be created by the group — each player could create a single ship — though the Gamemaster may choose to generate ships and let the Players select from the list. Collectively, these ships are a squadron. This is a term of convenience rather than a technically-accurate description of a particular ship group.

SQUADRON POINTS

The total number of ships in a squadron depends partly on the Scale of the ships: larger vessels are rare and require a greater resources from Starfleet, and are deployed sparingly. Similarly, highly-specialized vessels are much in demand, and are scarce and precious resources. A ship costs Squadron Points equal to its Scale, plus 1 for each Department with a score of 5.

Example: *Vice-Admiral Ross is gathering his squadron, the Seventh Tactical Wing. He selects the* U.S.S. Defiant *to be part of that squadron. The* Defiant *is Scale 3, and has a Security Department of 5, so it costs 4 Squadron Points.*

The Gamemaster determines how many Squadron Points can be spent on ships, usually between 12 and 30. The more points, the larger and more complex the squadron, and the more capable it is of facing large problems. It's probably better to start with a small point value, and give additional Squadron Points (and vessels) as the campaign progresses.

Upon squadron selection, the admiral should select a flagship where they will normally operate. This ship should have the highest command department and it receives a Trait of *Admiral X's Flagship*, where X is the admiral's name.

Each ship in the squadron generates its own Crew Support, which can be used to create and introduce Supporting

Characters from that ship. As noted above, when a Supporting Character is introduced, they may be assigned to any vacant role aboard the vessel. All the senior staff may be Supporting Characters, allowing play to move between different ships with their own crews.

In addition to Crew Support from vessels, the admiral's staff receive 3 Crew Support, to create and introduce Supporting Characters who work as the admiral's support staff rather than an individual ship's crew. Whenever a character in an Admiralty game takes the Supervisor Talent (page 136 of the *Star Trek Adventures* core rulebook), the player must choose to which pool of Crew Support the new Talent applies: the admiral's staff, or a squadron ship.

COMMAND IN PLAY

Each Discipline is an important part of a character's makeup, but what it signifies for any given character can vary. This section looks at what the Command Discipline may mean for a character at especially high or low ratings. These are suggestions, but may help Players visualize a character and how Disciplines reflect their nature.

COMMAND SCORE OF 1

The character has rudimentary training in the chain of command; basic skills with rhetoric, diplomacy, and negotiations; and a modest degree of personal discipline. They're unexceptional and unlikely to excel in situations that rely on Command. Unsure or awkward outside of their areas of expertise, they may simply be inexperienced and uncertain as to their authority and how far they can push others. They are ill-at-ease when giving orders.

The character might be socially awkward, anxious, or unconcerned with interpersonal matters, blunt, and might not communicate well outside their areas of expertise. They will struggle with situations where etiquette and diplomacy are valuable.

An undisciplined character might fall prey to distractions; have a poor sense of personal responsibility; be lazy; or be unsure of what motivates them. This may mean the character succumbs easily to outside influence, and lacks the resolve and mental fortitude to endure hardship or resist temptation.

Example: *Lieutenant Reg Barclay and Lieutenant Tom Paris are examples of characters with a Command Discipline of 1. Paris is socially adept, through personal charisma (his Presence Attribute, and Talents) rather than learned skill, but he's rash, irresponsible, and easily led astray. During his career he grows past these limitations (increases his Command Discipline). Barclay is an exceptional engineer whose neuroses and foibles have hindered his career.*

COMMAND SCORE OF 2 OR 3

The character is familiar with the chain of command, and is used to giving orders appropriate to their station and role. They're capable speakers, with enough knowledge of rhetoric, politics, and negotiation to help them in a peaceful missions and tense situations. They are also self-reliant and responsible.

COMMAND SCORE OF 4 OR 5

A talented leader, a skilled public speaker, and driven by a powerful sense of personal responsibility, the character displays qualities one thinks of when imagining a Starfleet captain.

The character knows how to lead; how to inspire people to overcome fatigue or fear; brings out the best of their subordinates; and turns a crew from a group of individuals into a team greater than the sum of its parts, The character is well-versed in rhetoric, diplomacy, and politics, with perhaps a passion for history, the arts, philosophy, political discourse, or a related field that brings a flourish to their speeches.

Easily described as dutiful, the character's' sense of responsibility and personal discipline makes them self-reliant, seldom doubting their purpose or resolve. Even if they do, they act effectively despite such vulnerabilities. They may be seen as stubborn or intractable, but this isn't entirely accurate. It would be correct to say that they do not change their minds needlessly.

OTHER DISCIPLINES

As a single Discipline can define a character's identity in a variety of interesting ways, combinations of Disciplines can provide interesting context. The character's two highest Disciplines can be a definitive part of how they approach problems.

CONN

The character is Starfleet through-and-through and was born for starship command. Natural explorers and pioneers, these characters take after the test pilots and astronauts of the past. Well-versed in the traditions and procedures of Starfleet, they have an in-depth understanding of protocol. An extensive knowledge of ship and fleet capabilities is combined with leadership expertise and a decisive manner to put all that knowledge to use. This isn't an uncommon combination. Many starship captains began their career at the helm, though they don't all maintain their piloting skills.

Example: *Jonathan Archer, captain of the* Enterprise *NX-01 and a former test pilot, and Hikaru Sulu, U.S.S. Enterprise helmsman and captain of the U.S.S. Excelsior, are both examples of characters with high Command and high Conn.*

ENGINEERING

The character has enormous technical expertise, and knows their ship inside out. A capable leader, they have likely spent time in charge of large numbers of engineers. Their organizational and interpersonal skills make them valuable chief engineers and project leaders, while their technical skills give them insight into the tools at their disposal and how best to use them.

Example: Benjamin Sisko spent several years leading starship development teams at the Utopia Planitia Fleet Yards; he is an example of a character with high Command and high Engineering, during at least part of his career. Similarly, Montgomery Scott and Charles 'Trip' Tucker III are engineers and capable leaders, and who took command of their ships when required.

SECURITY

The character is a battlefield leader, a skilled tactician, an accomplished strategist, or a talented investigator. These characters lead away missions, fight battles, and deal with life-or-death situations. They tend to rise to prominence during times of strife and conflict, and are also likely to be physical, energetic individuals, accustomed to leading from the front.

Example: James Kirk is a character with high Command and high Security. Worf, son of Mogh, and Kira Nerys are also good examples, combining a sense of duty and an engagement in politics with martial and strategic skill.

SCIENCE

The character is driven by a need to explore and understand the diverse universe, inspiring others to do the same. Well-read in a range of scientific fields, they spark equal curiosity in subordinates. They also have the discipline to scrutinize their own theories rigorously; the organizational skill to lead collaborations between specialists from different fields; and the persuasiveness to explain the virtue of a particular avenue of study or research mission.

Example: Jean-Luc Picard, captain of the Enterprise-D and Enterprise-E, and Kathryn Janeway, captain of the U.S.S. Voyager, both have high Command and high Science, though their fields of expertise differ. Spock is also this kind of character, especially later in his career.

MEDICINE

The character is an accomplished healer — a doctor, counselor or expert in some field of medical practice — and leader. Commonly found in authority at medical institutions such as large hospitals or medical ships, they may have been a starship chief medical officer, with a staff of several doctors, nurses and orderlies. Practical skills plus administrative and organizational talent are vital, often resulting in crisis relief missions.

CREATING COMMAND CHARACTERS

The following are suggestions for players creating command characters, usually the Commanding Officer or executive officer:

LIFEPATH STEP ONE
Any species can serve in a command role, though different species have different styles of leadership. Species that offer increased Presence may be especially effective leaders.

LIFEPATH STEP TWO
At this stage, the *Homeworld*, *Busy Colony*, or *Starship or Starbase* options might improve Command, though Command can be improved later if another choice is made.

LIFEPATH STEP THREE
In step three, the *Starfleet*, *Business or Trade*, *Artistic and Creative*, and *Diplomacy and Politics* options can all increase Command, providing a Focus to help develop and specialize the character.

LIFEPATH STEP FOUR
At the Academy, the Command Track is the natural choice for a command character, providing a significant increase to Command, as well as three Focuses and a single Talent. All can shape the character's abilities.

LIFEPATH STEP FIVE
At this step, the Young Officer option is unlikely to be appropriate as few are given significant leadership roles when young. Many first-time commanding officers and executive officers will take the Experienced Officer option: they're seasoned enough for a senior position — Kirk, Sisko, and Janeway are examples — while the most experienced are Veteran Officers, like Picard.

LIFEPATH STEP SIX
Here, a number of Career Events can increase Command, although this is more to add character flavor, perhaps showing the events that led to a current rank and position.

LIFEPATH STEP SEVEN
With finishing touches, the character's Attributes and Disciplines can be fine-tuned to fit a particular vision. Once complete, select a role.

Example: Beverly Crusher, chief medical officer of the Enterprise-D, Enterprise-E, and former head of Starfleet Medical, is a character with high Command and high Medicine. Deanna Troi is a different type, using her training as a counselor to assist during diplomatic missions.

This section provides a selection of Focuses that may be particularly useful or interesting for a command officer, and a brief discussion of what a Focus represents or how it could be used. Focuses are not necessary: a character can know about any of these areas of expertise without having an associated Focus. Having the Focus indicates an ability to gain 2 successes when rolling equal to or under Command Discipline when a focused area of expertise is relevant.

Deliberately, and as in real life, there is overlap between different Focuses. Different fields of study and expertise inform one another, and individuals may develop similar skills from differing origins.

- **Art:** The character is highly knowledgeable about art; how it reflects its culture; individual pieces and artist history; and theories and analyses of pieces' meanings. They draw upon this knowledge when attempting to be inspiring, or persuasive, or trying to reach an audience. Effective where an audience is familiar with a work or style, some artistic sensibilities do not translate between species. This Focus could be renamed for specific art disciplines and specific cultures' arts. Literature and performing arts, such as quoting epic poetry or Shakespeare (in English or Klingon), mark a character as cultured.

- **Composure:** The character is good at remaining calm, useful where clear-headedness is needed. It is also vital when not revealing feelings or thoughts to an adversary by maintaining a 'poker face'. Vulcans, for example, have the discipline and emotional suppression to remain impassive during traumatic situations.

- **Cultural Studies:** The character has knowledge of many cultures. This is helpful when dealing with members of familiar cultures, or when explaining cultural nuances to someone unfamiliar with them. It may also be renamed to reflect a narrower, deeper study of a single or small number of related cultures. The Gamemaster should reward successful knowledge- or observation-related Tasks with in-depth information.

FOCUSES AS PASTIMES

Focuses can represent hobbies of Main Characters, denoting amateur expertise. Hobbies provide the Gamemaster with some great scenes when starting a mission or session: captains practicing an instrument, reading cultural texts, viewing a seminar via subspace transmission, or engaging in a debate in a holodeck simulation.

- **Debate:** The character is skilled in debate and discussion, presenting ideas in a compelling, succinct manner, using all the tools of rhetoric and oration and is skilled at defending or dissecting ideas. This is appropriate for Tellarite characters (among others) who revel in argument and believe good ideas must withstand scrutiny.

- **Deception:** The character is a talented liar, and capable of spotting the same in others. Starfleet does not condone deception; it is a matter of pride that Starfleet officers do not lie. But even if officers are true to themselves and speak honestly when it counts, calculated deception is a necessary tactic. Of course, knowing how to lie is an important part of spotting when others might be lying.

- **Diplomacy:** The character is versed in diplomatic matters on the grand scale of international relations, alliances, treaties and agreements, and at a personal level to settle conflicts. Diplomatic characters understand how nations interact and they are expert in defusing tensions and de-escalating hostilities between groups by seeking common ground or mutual advantage. Characters with this Focus are suited to first contact missions and situations where arranging cooperation is essential.

- **Empathy:** The character is sensitive to others' emotions and perspectives, and gains valuable insights into others reactions. Spotting and understanding emotional and personal issues can help them overcome problems. This is a vital part of a Counsellor's responsibilities, but it is also useful for command officers, as leadership requires an understanding of people.

- **Gambling:** The character has a knack for evaluating odds and knowing which chances to take. They might be accustomed to games like poker, or the Ferengi dabo and tongo, where both luck and skill are needed. Not unheard of amongst Starfleet officers — weighing up a perilous situation is important as long as leaders take responsibility for the consequences — such characters may have the *Bold* Talent (page 135 of the ***Star Trek Adventures*** *core rulebook*) to reflect their willingness to take chances.

- **History:** The character is well-versed in history, with a broad overview or a specific fascination with a single era; one world or a culture's history; or a type of history such as military history or the history of exploration. The past can have useful parallels to today, and can help when avoiding repeated mistakes. As with Cultural Studies, this Focus may be renamed to reflect the character's knowledge: a character with a Focus of *History* may have a broad understanding of the past, while a character with *21st Century Earth History* will know about events and people specific to that era.

- **Inspiration:** The character is an inspiration to others, helping them overcome fears and doubts during a crisis. Even Starfleet officers, determined as they are, rely on inspiring leadership in difficult situations. An inspirational character can get the most from subordinates, reinvigorating the weary and rallying the demoralized. Inspiring characters are often vital where the stakes are high and success seems distant.

- **Law:** The character has studied the Federation legal code, and laws of other cultures too, and is expert enough to provide counsel during trials, or pass judgement in criminal matters. Command officers should understand Federation law or Starfleet regulations, and may serve as advocates in court. Characters with this Focus know the law, understand of procedure and practice, and can give sound legal advice.

- **Lead by Example:** The character excels at leading by doing, and 'gets their hands dirty'. They do not sit back and delegate, and never give an order they would not follow. These are practical leaders unafraid to test their own skills and who expect subordinates to follow without hesitation. Characters with this Focus have moved to the command department from some other part of Starfleet, and are used to relying on their own skills rather than directing others.

- **Linguistics:** The character has a broad knowledge of communication and fluency in several languages. Despite the universal translator people still study languages, partly in case of technical faults or encounters with unfamiliar cultures, and partly because language is an important expression of cultural and societal evolution. Early in Starfleet history, ships often carried linguists to expand the universal translator and help communicate with unfamiliar cultures.

- **Mental Discipline:** The character has learned to control their thoughts, emotions and even parts of their subconscious. Mental discipline is rare and needs considerable effort to learn, but it offers an invaluable defense against telepathic intrusion. It is a bulwark against fear, panic, and despair, aids the recall of details, and allows tasks to be done despite distractions like pain. Vulcans, particularly those who have undergone the ritual of *Kolinahr*, are likely to have this Focus, but they are not the only ones. Cardassians are often trained in childhood giving them eidetic memories, and allowing them to attempt protection from telepaths.

- **Negotiation:** The character is a deal-maker, finding mutual advantage — or the appearance of it — in all manner of social situations. Negotiation frequently involves trade or resource distribution, and those involved seek an outcome that both sides find

The universal translator was invented shortly before 2151, and was experimental when the *Enterprise* NX-01 launched. During this time (and into the mid-23rd Century) xenolinguists on starships were relied on for communication and characters from these eras are likely to have a Xenolinguistics Focus.

acceptable. Building trust between parties can be a slow process best handled by a meticulous approach. Ferengi are notorious for their enthusiasm for negotiation, but also for their tendency to deceive others to get a better deal.

- **Philosophy:** The character ponders the nature of knowledge, reality, existence, and semantics. This is a complex subject, with countless schools of thought and each culture contains numerous philosophies. This Focus may indicate that the character has studied many different schools of thought, or it may be renamed to indicate the character's deep study of a single philosophy. For example, a character could study *Vulcan Philosophy*, considering the teachings of Surak, the principles of logic and emotional control. Philosophy applies to Tasks where a character tries to understand a problem, or needs to determine an approach to the problem. It may also apply during social conflicts when attempting to explain matters effectively.

- **Politics:** The character understands how societies are structured and run, and the ideologies that can influence them. This includes the Federation's democratic values, but also theories behind other cultures and regimes. It covers internal dynamics that create laws that shape society. This Focus is most valuable when studying or discussing different forms of society and government, such as during debates over whether a course of action contravenes a society's mores. Characters with an interest in politics often find themselves supporting an admiral (or promoted to admiral themselves), where understanding the political landscape is a useful survival skill.

- **Strategy/Tactics:** The character is a skilled in deploying ships and soldiers, and in coordinating the application of force from many sources. They have an appreciation of past tacticians and strategists, and have studied significant battles. They may also have a talent for games of strategy, such as chess or Stratagema. This Focus is useful when creating Advantages related to a battle plan or maneuver, or when giving bonuses

Command characters will usually set out a strategy as one part of ongoing activities within a scene. This might be the breakdown of work within a group, so that everyone knows what they have to do, or additional coordination and preparation so that everyone knows to do X when Y happens. In combat, plans might be conveyed by hand signals, or by mentioning an attack drill prepared and practiced in advance, allowing decisive orders with little effort.

Generally, these sorts of activities work just like any other activity in *Star Trek Adventures*. Planning and coordination of others, or a rousing speech to inspire, is likely to be a Command Task with a Difficulty of 0 (increase Difficulty based on how difficult it is to communicate) simply to generate Momentum. In this case, any Momentum generated is from the fruits of coordination and planning, or the extra motivation everyone has received. More specific plans may be represented by taking a Task or spending Momentum to create an Advantage, with the Advantage representing the specific orders given. These could be a specific instructions, precision timing, and command judgements to make the impossible possible, or the difficult easier. Advantages representing strategies should only last a brief time — one round — as they quickly lose their relevance as circumstances change.

in combat. Characters often have a high Security Discipline, but not always: excellent strategists do not always need personal combat skills.

- **Teaching:** The character is a capable instructor, providing guidance and knowledge to others. Characters best-suited to teaching related to other Focuses, but they can teach anything they know to others. Teaching is especially suitable as a Focus for Tasks that provide assistance to allies, and characters with a Teaching Focus are suited to Talents that give them further benefits when offering aid.

- **Team Dynamics:** The character has a deep understanding of how groups interact and how best to gain the best results through cooperation. This applies to small teams, rather than a starship's entire crew, as not all team dynamics scale easily. This Focus can activate when laying out a plan for a group working on a complex project (which could be a Challenge or Extended Task), or when assisting or providing a bonus on Tasks towards a group effort.

COMMAND TALENTS

This section provides additional Talents suited to command officers and characters with a high Command Discipline score. Each Talent may only be selected once unless otherwise noted. Players are free to rename the Talents they select to suit their own tastes and the backgrounds of their characters. This will not affect the rules for a Talent.

BARGAIN
REQUIREMENTS: Command 3+
When negotiating an offer with someone during Social Conflict, you may re-roll a d20 on your next *Persuade* Task to convince that person. If the Social Conflict involves an Extended Task, you gain the *Progression 1* (page 91 of the *Star Trek Adventures* core rulebook) benefit when you roll your Challenge Dice.

CALL OUT TARGETS
REQUIREMENT: Command 3+, Security 3+
Upon assisting a character making an attack (using either the *Assist* Task, the *Direct* Task, or some other means), the helped character generates one point of bonus Momentum if they succeed; bonus Momentum cannot be saved to the group pool.

CALL TO ACTION
REQUIREMENT: Command 3+
In a Conflict, a character may use the *Prepare* Minor Action to grant one ally a Minor Action of their choice (performed immediately) if they can communicate with that ally.

COLD READING
REQUIREMENT: Command 4+
Succeeding at a Task during Social Conflict generates one bonus Momentum which must be used for the *Obtain Information* Momentum Spend to gain knowledge about an individual on the other side of the interaction. If the Social Conflict involves an Extended Task, the character gains the *Scrutinize 1* benefit (see page 91 of the *Star Trek Adventures* core rulebook) when rolling Challenge Dice.

COORDINATED EFFORTS
REQUIREMENT: Command 4+
During an Extended Task, an assisted character may gain either the Scrutinize 2 or Progression 1 benefits (see page 91 of the *core rulebook*) when they roll their Challenge Dice.

DECISIVE LEADERSHIP
REQUIREMENT: Command 4+
In a Conflict, whenever the character performs the *Assist* Task and would then pay two Momentum to keep the initiative, the cost to keep the initiative is reduced to 0.

FLEET COMMANDER

REQUIREMENT: Command 4+

Commanding a vessel during a fleet action reduces the Difficulty of a Task to grant a bonus to your vessel or group by 1, to a minimum of 1. Aboard a vessel during a fleet action, the character may treat the vessel as having a Command Department of 4+, regardless of the actual value.

MULTI-DISCIPLINE

REQUIREMENTS: Command 3+; Not Commanding Officer or Admiral

The character may select one additional Role, but not Commanding Officer or Admiral.

PLAN OF ACTION

REQUIREMENT: Command 4+

When an ally succeeds at a Task that was made possible or had reduced Difficulty because of an Advantage created by the character, if that Advantage represented a plan or strategy, they generate two bonus Momentum. Bonus Momentum cannot be saved into the group pool.

TIME MANAGEMENT

REQUIREMENT: Command 4+

During any Challenge, Extended Task or other activity under time pressure, the character may attempt a Control + Command Task with a Difficulty 3. If this Task succeeds, reduce the total number of intervals the Players have taken by 1; for every 2 Momentum spent (Repeatable) reduce by a further 1. The character has managed to minimize lost time. If the Task fails, add one additional interval as the character's efforts actually waste time.

COMMAND DIVISION CHARACTERS
PILOTING THROUGH THE STARS

AT THE HELM

Simply put, a conn officer is the officer physically at the controls of a vessel, whether as pilot of a shuttle or fighter, or as the flight controller of a massive starship. These officers are more than just pilots. Most conn officers are young, and often aspiring command personnel, studying Starfleet operations and procedures first-hand from the bridge, observing experienced officers and learning the nuances and intricacies of life amongst the stars.

A conn officer is expected to be a jack-of-all-trades, with a grounding in science, engineering, combat, Starfleet procedures, and the tradition and culture of exploratory space travel. This requires familiarity with starships: an understanding of the ships they served aboard, but also the capabilities of other cultures' ships. They have a knack for operating in extreme or unusual environments, and as conn officers learn their trade with shuttles or fighters, they know how to operate an EV suit, and move around in zero-gravity conditions.

Whatever their postings, conn officers need to be knowledgeable, broadly skilled, and have flexibility in meeting many challenges. They often move departments later in their careers, becoming a new generation of command officers.

CONN IN PLAY

Each Discipline is an important part of a character's makeup, and what a given Discipline's rating means differ for each character. This section looks at what the Discipline may mean for a character at high or low ratings. These are suggestions, but they may help Players visualize characters and how their Disciplines reflect their nature.

CONN SCORE OF 1

The character has basic training in piloting and starship operations because their work is elsewhere. While they may be capable of piloting a shuttle, or helming a starship, they shouldn't be expected pull off complex maneuvers, do much more than plot a basic course, and keep an eye on the controls. The character is likely to be uncomfortable in zero-G and is ill-suited to extra-vehicular activities.

With little grounding in the procedures of starship life, they are unaware of ideas and traditions that are second nature to their colleagues. The character is in Starfleet because of their skills, but probably did not expect a starship posting. In some cases, the character may have never attended Starfleet Academy, instead gaining a commission later in life.

Example: *Leonard McCoy and Deanna Troi are good examples of characters with a Conn of 1. Their duties don't need familiarity with starship operations. McCoy studied medicine as a civilian and joined Starfleet in later life, receiving a commission to match his authority. Troi attended Starfleet Academy but her focus was on psychology, psychiatry, and diplomacy; this changed later in her career when she took the bridge officer's exam and was promoted to Commander rank. Starfleet attracts scientists who want resources and support or who need experience from service, but they may have little interest in serving aboard a Starship. This makes them good examples of characters with Conn 1.*

CREATING CONN CHARACTERS

These are suggestions for players wishing to create conn characters, typically Flight Controllers. They may fit other roles depending on their Disciplines:

LIFEPATH STEP ONE
Any species can take the helm, though different species tend towards differing activities under that heading. Species that offer Control tend to be excellent pilots.

LIFEPATH STEP TWO
At this stage, the *Frontier Colony* and *Starship or Starbase* options both have the possibility to improve Conn, though there will be opportunities to improve later if another option is chosen.

LIFEPATH STEP THREE
In step three, the *Starfleet*, *Agriculture or Rural*, *Science and Technology*, and *Diplomacy and Politics* options can all increase a character's Conn, and give a Focus to develop and specialize the character.

LIFEPATH STEP FOUR
At the Academy, the Command Track is the natural option for a conn character, providing a significant increase to Conn, three Focuses, and a single Talent. All can shape the character's abilities in major ways.

LIFEPATH STEP FIVE
At this step, the Young Officer option may be appropriate. Many conn officers are juniors on their first posting after the Academy: inexperienced but eager to learn. This doesn't rule out experienced conn officers.

LIFEPATH STEP SIX
There are a number of Career Events that can increase Conn, but this is an opportunity to add flavor to the character, perhaps showing events leading to the character's current rank and position.

LIFEPATH STEP SEVEN
These finishing touches fine tune the character's Attributes and Disciplines to fit a particular vision. After this, select a role. For a conn officer, this is often Flight Controller but, depending on other Disciplines, they may be suited to other roles as well.

CONN SCORE OF 2 OR 3
The character has a solid proficiency in starship operations, helm control, navigation, extra-vehicular activities, and is familiar with the traditions and practicalities of space exploration. It also shows understanding of current and historical starship design.

CONN SCORE OF 4 OR 5
These character are expert pilots, who can pull off maneuvers that others would see as too risky or difficult, and are familiar with the intricacies of stellar cartography and astronavigation allowing them to use or avoid stellar phenomena to chart efficient courses while keeping ships safe. They understand propulsion systems and starship design in general, only being surpassed by dedicated engineers, vital knowledge for getting the best out of a ship under any conditions. They are accustomed to operating in non-standard gravity, particularly zero-g, and are experts with environmental suits and similar equipment, having little difficulty moving and operating outside a ship.

These characters will also know the history and traditions of Starfleet, and the ships and organizations of other fleets. This expertise in ship and fleet capabilities make these characters real assets on the bridge, able to judge and anticipate how other vessels will act during a crisis, and able to provide advice (or take the initiative) accordingly.

OTHER DISCIPLINES

Just as a single Discipline can define who a character is in a variety of interesting ways, so too can different combinations of Disciplines, providing interesting and valuable context for a character. In particular, the character's two highest Disciplines can be a definitive part of how the character approaches problems.

COMMAND
This is covered in depth on page 40 in the Command in Play section.

ENGINEERING

These characters are experts in building, maintaining, and repairing engine systems from the perspective of flying a ship. Often serving aboard pathfinder and test-bed vessels, these characters also have the skills to operate advanced propulsion and navigation systems. They are valued test-pilots and often work closely with starship designers.

Example: *Tom Paris is a good example of a character with high Conn and Engineering Disciplines, demonstrated during his time aboard the U.S.S. Voyager when he led design of the Delta Flyer shuttle. Wesley Crusher is another example, although his career is very brief, possessing an exceptional aptitude for engineering, and receiving extensive training in helm operations before and during his time at Starfleet Academy.*

SECURITY

These characters lean towards combat operations and perilous situations, flying a transport shuttle while under fire, piloting attack fighters, and similar. On some vessels, particularly in the 23rd Century, helm officers and navigators would be responsible for tactical systems, requiring officers who were competent in both Disciplines.

Example: *Pavel Chekov served for many years as the navigator of the U.S.S. Enterprise, and then as chief of security. Ro Laren served as the conn officer of the Enterprise-D, and qualified for advanced tactical training. Both are characters with high Conn and Security Disciplines.*

SCIENCE

The character has extensive knowledge of spatial phenomena, including the fields relating to subspace. This expands upon the character's existing understanding of astronavigation and stellar cartography. The character is skilled at navigating the most perilous regions, and can chart the best route through unknown space. Such characters are often natural explorers: scientific curiosity and the skill to take a starship beyond any frontier are a powerful combination.

Example: *Jadzia Dax is a highly competent pilot, often serving at the helm of the Defiant, and a dedicated and talented scientist. Dax gained this expertise in the years before she became Joined. She's a character with high Conn and Science Disciplines.*

MEDICINE

Pilots with medical training, or medics trained to fly spacecraft, can be extremely valuable aboard emergency response vessels: ambulance and evacuation shuttles and runabouts, are more effective if those on board are trained for both flight and medicine. Conn is invaluable to medics and physicians who operate in unusual environments: zero-G medicine is complicated.

Example: *The nearest example is Tom Paris, who served as a field medic in addition to being senior flight controller. This was necessity rather than medical expertise: Paris had rudimentary life sciences training.*

CONN FOCUSES

This selection of Focuses (with brief descriptions) may be useful or interesting for a conn officer. Focuses are not mandatory: characters can have understanding or expertise without the associated Focus, but having a Focus indicates a particular emphasis on a particular area.

There is a degree of overlap between Focuses, and this is deliberate. Just as in real life, fields of study and areas of expertise overlap, and individuals end up with similar skills even if they came to them by different routes:

- **Astronavigation:** The character is an expert at interpreting and studying star charts, and picking the best route through a region. Space is not an empty void, and astronavigation requires understanding of subspace fluctuations, gas density variations, cosmic background radiation, gravitational distortions caused by stars and singularities, and a bewildering variety of factors that can change journey times by days, weeks or even months.

- **Astrophysics:** The character understands how stellar bodies interact, and the theories that underpin spatial phenomena such as stars, black holes, nebulae, dark matter, and dark energy. This is useful for Starfleet officers to understand but it has particular significance for scientists, and for conn officers navigating the stars. Astrophysics and astronavigation overlap, but this covers the theoretical underpinnings of reality.

- **Atmospheric Flight:** The character excels at operating aircraft and small spacecraft in an atmosphere. Atmospheric pressure, air resistance, wind speed and gravity make atmospheric flight different to spaceflight, and understanding those differences can have a considerable impact when flying in rough conditions. Anyone trained to fly a shuttlecraft has basic atmospheric flight training, but to Focus in this field allows a pilot to brave a storm, or out-fly a pursuer, inside an atmosphere.

- **Combat Maneuvers:** The character has special training for flying in battle. This involves evading enemy fire, moving to maximize the tactical officer's chances of hitting a target, moving as part of combat formations, and navigating crowded and chaotic battles. Combat maneuvers depend on the size and agility of a ship. Massive vessels like *Galaxy*-class starships are fast, but their size means that they're used to shield smaller

ENGAGE!

Conn characters are responsible for getting a ship where it needs to go, and this can be a passive task unless the Gamemaster puts obstacles and challenges in the way. Going from A to B at warp 4 isn't interesting, but it is what a flight controller does and it gives them few opportunities to show their prowess or stand out.

Usually it doesn't matter how fast a ship is travelling beyond "at warp", "at impulse", "using thrusters". Vessels fly at "story plot speed", and travel just quickly enough to get to their destination just in time for interesting things to happen. The Gamemaster can involve conn officers by asking the conn officer to decide how much Power they want to spend on going to warp, and then adjusting events upon arrival according to how much is used (more power = a faster journey). If there's a known peril or combat at the other end of the journey, this is an interesting choice because using too much power reaching the action can leave a ship struggling when it arrives. In such a case, treat the decision to go to warp and what happens when it arrives as the same scene.

As a rule of thumb, 1 Power spent on warp travel represents travelling at warp 1, 2 Power is warp 2, and so on. This isn't a perfect solution: ships with 10 Power or more cannot travel at warp 10 or above, but higher expenditures can represent

fractional factors above warp 9 if the Gamemaster sees fit. The Gamemaster may require a minimum amount of Power be spent for a journey (the Players can always spend more) to ensure that the ship reaches its destination in ample time for the plot; responding to a distress call at warp 2 may well mean that the ship arrives days too late to be of any help.

The Gamemaster may ask for a simple (Difficulty 0, 1, or 2) **Reason + Conn Task** to plot a course, and this can jump-start a situation. Momentum generated here nicely represents how promptly a ship arrives and the benefits of reaching a destination quickly; Complications can help set up the challenges to come. In combat too, a conn officer may still roll even if the Tasks themselves are Difficulty 0: piloting is the kind of activity where knowing how well you succeeded, and passing on that success to crewmates, is entirely justified.

And while **Star Trek** brought us the transporter, there's no reason why Player Characters cannot use shuttles to travel back and forth, another opportunity for a conn officer. Indeed, because a **Star Trek Adventures** game doesn't have the budgetary and production design concerns of a **Star Trek** episode, film and TV production limitations that prevented shuttles appearing regularly don't exist for the Player Characters. This book includes additional small craft for skilled conn officers.

vessels, or to anchor a battle line, rather than to fly a precise course through the heart of the enemy line.

- **Evasive Action:** A character skilled in evasive actions keeps the ship safe and intact. Quick reflexes, sound judgement, and an instinct for maneuvering allow threats to be countered as they emerge. In battle this is invaluable, but it is also useful avoiding unknown conditions during space exploration.

- **Extra-Vehicular Activity:** These characters have logged hundreds (possibly thousands) of hours in environmental suits and thruster suits. They can use and maintain all common, contemporary forms of environmental suit (with variable configurations depending on conditions). Familiar with moving, working, and even fighting in low-G and micro-gravity, the character never feels nauseous.

- **Ground Vehicles:** While ground vehicles are not commonplace thanks to transporters and simple aircraft, the character can operate and maintain them. This expertise also includes the history of such vehicles, as many of them are historical objects in their own right. While this may seem irrelevant in Starfleet, some planetary conditions make ground transport a necessity, and a few exploratory and combat vessels produced all-terrain vehicles for use when needed.

- **Helm Operations:** The character has a deep understanding of how a starship responds to inputs and commands, and can use that to get the best from the quirks and peculiarities of an individual ship. This includes learning response rates; the precise interactions of thrust, inertia and mass; ships clearances in turns; the time to reach a warp factor; and all the tiny details that separate triumph and tragedy. This Focus doesn't cover small craft (see below); it is for general-purpose starship piloting.

- **Impulse Engines:** The character knows how to get the best from impulse engines and that a rudimentary plasma/fusion thrust system, combined with a low-intensity subspace field, amplifies the propulsive effect. This is used for most sub-light maneuvering, but not for fine maneuvers or anything approaching lightspeed. The character's expertise covers flight at Impulse speed, and also gives understanding of the Impulse mechanisms, allowing maintenance and repairs.

- **Small Craft:** The character flies shuttles, runabouts, and fighters as if they were an extensions of their own body. These handle differently from starships and, while this doesn't matter during routine flights, skill with small craft can be the difference between life and death in a crisis. Many small craft need only one or two flight crew, so this Focus cover operations, tactical Tasks, engineering problems, and the to-be-expected piloting and navigation.

- **Starfleet Protocols:** The character has an in-depth knowledge of Starfleet protocols, regulations, and procedures. This Focus gives the sort of legalistic knowledge useful in untangling tricky regulations in sticky situations.

- **Starship Recognition:** The character has a broad knowledge of different classes and types of starship, and can recognize them by visual appearance, thermal and radiation emissions, and by a number of other indicators. This is not just useful trivia, as the character can spot deviations from an expected baseline and so is able to identify, for example, when a ship has been modified or is producing false signals.

- **Survival:** The character can use their knowledge of travel and navigation to help survival in the wilderness. Understanding how to navigate by the stars is not wildly dissimilar to understanding how find a way out of a forest or desert, if the character knows the environmental variables. With this training a pilot who can fly through nebulae and around black holes can use the principles to find a way through a wilderness.

- **Warp Drive:** The character has extensive knowledge of warp drives, the means of faster-than-light travel for all known Alpha and Beta Quadrant cultures including the Federation. This Focus covers warp drive from the pilot's perspective: how a warp field configuration interacts with subspace variations, local gravity, and other spatial effects; and the trade-off between speed and power consumption for warp journeys. It also includes hands-on expertise so that the character can repair and maintain warp drives.

CONN TALENTS

This section provides a selection of additional Talents for conn officers and others with a high Conn score. Each Talent may only be selected once unless otherwise noted. Players are free to rename the Talents to suit their own tastes and their characters' backgrounds. This will not affect the rules in any way.

ATTACK RUN
REQUIREMENT: Conn 4+
A success in the *Attack Pattern* Task lets a character spend two Momentum. Enemy Attacks against the character's ship do not reduce in Difficulty due to the *Attack Pattern* Task.

COVERING ADVANCE
REQUIREMENT: Conn 3+
A success at any Helm Task means two Momentum can be spent to block a single enemy vessel within Medium range, plus one additional enemy vessel for each additional Momentum spent beyond that (Repeatable). When a blocked

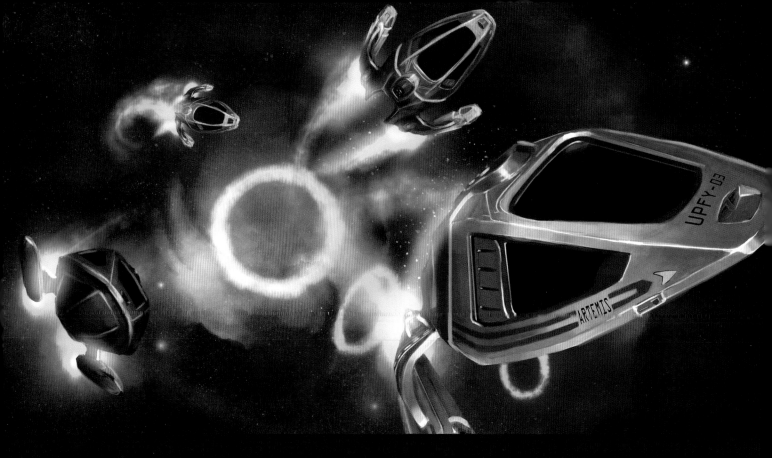

vessel makes its next attack, before the beginning of the character's next Turn, the Difficulty of any Attack that does not target your vessel has a base Difficulty equal to the character ship's Scale, instead of normal Difficulty.

EFFICIENT EVASION

REQUIREMENT: Conn 3+
Attempting an *Evasive Action* Task for the second or subsequent time in a row during a scene reduces the Power Requirement for *Evasive Action* to 0.

FLIGHT CONTROLLER

REQUIREMENT: Flight controller role
Whenever the character assists an NPC in a Conn Task, one d20 re-roll may be done. The second result must be used.

GLANCING IMPACT

REQUIREMENT: Conn 4+
Succeeding at the *Evasive Action* Task increases the Resistance of the ship being piloted by +2. This bonus lasts until the start of the character's next Turn.

INERTIA

REQUIREMENT: Conn 3+
When the character succeeds at a *Maneuver* Task, 1 Momentum may be spent to move one additional zone so long as the previous Turn included an *Impulse* or *Warp* Task.

MULTI-TASKING

REQUIREMENT: Conn 3+
Attempting the *Override* Task while at a bridge station including Helm and/or Navigator positions utilizes the character's Conn Discipline instead of the Discipline normally required for the Task.

PATHFINDER

REQUIREMENT: Conn 4+
When a character attempts a Task to plot a course through unknown territory, reduce the Difficulty of the Task by 1, 2, or 3, to a minimum of 1. Each point that reduces Difficulty increases the Complication Range of the Task.

PRECISION MANEUVERING

REQUIREMENT: Conn 4+
Reduces the Difficulty of the Task by 1, to a minimum of 0, when attempting a Task that requires precise maneuvering, or where there is a collision risk.

SPACEWALK

REQUIREMENT: Conn 3+
Whenever the Difficulty of a Task is increased thanks to low- or zero-gravity, ignore the increase. A Task that is normally possible but isn't because of low- or zero-gravity, may be attempted at +1 Difficulty to the Task.

STRAFING RUN

REQUIREMENT: Conn 4+
When a character succeeds at the *Attack Pattern* Task and spends Momentum to keep the initiative, the cost to keep the initiative is 0.

CHAPTER 04.00

FEDERATION VESSELS

572821400412
3985104697936745

FEDERATION VESSELS
FEDERATION STARSHIPS

"AND ALL I ASK IS A TALL SHIP AND A STAR TO STEER HER BY."

— CAPTAIN JAMES T. KIRK, QUOTING JOHN MASEFIELD

THE FLEET

In this chapter you will find information and statistics for 16 Federation starships, supplementing those presented in the **Star Trek Adventures** core rulebook. Any of these vessels are suited for characters to serve on, and most characters will have served on board one of these vessels some time in their past if they are of a higher rank. In the Original Series, it would have been common for officers to have served on *Daedalus* class vessels before moving onto newer designs, and *Nebula* class starships were often seen as a stepping stone to service on a *Galaxy*. Feel free to include these ships in the background of your campaign or even as your characters' hero ship.

DAEDALUS CLASS
ENTERED SERVICE: 2140

OVERVIEW: Previous to the Earth-Romulan War, Starfleet needed a large vessel to help protect and patrol the few trade lanes and colonies United Earth had set up. The *Daedalus* class was designed to fill that role using the least amount of resources and the lowest amount of advanced technology as possible. The development and success of the *NX* class made the Admiralty begin to pull *Daedalus*-class ships back to the Sol System for possible decommissioning, but the Earth-Romulan War gave this vessel new life through Starfleet's desperate need for vessels, allowing them to remain active until the late 2190s, with some being used even into the mid-23rd century.

CAPABILITIES: The low-tech design of the *Daedalus* class was due to its role as an escort for trade vessels and colony ships as well as routine scientific surveys, meaning its capabilities didn't have to be exceptional. At maximum speed, the class could barely achieve warp 4 and its under-powered impulse deck struggled at sublight speeds. The spaceframe itself was rudimentary with a simple cylinder

for its engineering section and a sphere for the command section. The weapon systems that it carried were also primitive with first generation phase cannons and guided missiles with thermonuclear payloads. The *Daedalus* class's primitive systems proved its success in the early years of the Earth-Romulan War when it was seen that Starfleet could build nearly four *Daedalus*-class vessels in the same amount of time as an *NX* class. Additionally, the primitive systems proved to be incredibly easy for even a moderately experienced crew to maintain and repair. Minor upgrades near the end of the war gave these starships greater capabilities by replacing the nuclear weapons with photonic torpedoes and replacing the sensor suites onboard with state-of-the-art systems produced in conjunction with the Vulcans and Andorians. So many of these vessels were constructed by the end of the war that Starfleet mothballed half of them to be used as 'hanger queens' to make repair and refits of the still active vessels that much easier. Over its decades of service, *Daedalus*-class vessels saw dozens of minor and major refits that allowed them to continue active service in Starfleet until the limitations of the spaceframe became apparent when increasing hostilities with the Klingon Empire in the 2250s and '60s showed the vulnerability of the design. Starfleet quickly phased them out of active duty to be replaced by *Constitution* and *Hermes*-class starships.

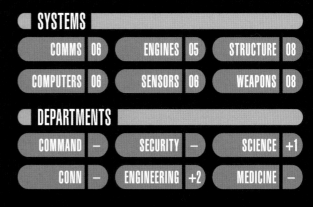

SYSTEMS

COMMS	06	ENGINES	05	STRUCTURE	08
COMPUTERS	06	SENSORS	06	WEAPONS	08

DEPARTMENTS

COMMAND	—	SECURITY	—	SCIENCE	+1
CONN	—	ENGINEERING	+2	MEDICINE	—

SCALE: 3

ATTACKS:

- Pulse Cannons
- Spatial Torpedoes
- Grappler Cable (Strength 2)

TALENTS

Daedalus-class starships have the following Talents:

- Polarized Hull Plating
- Grappler Cable
- Rugged Design

Due to their simple systems and adaptable construction, a Daedalus-class vessel may have up five Talents, rather than the three its Scale would normally permit.

NX CLASS
ENTERED SERVICE: 2151

OVERVIEW: In the decades before the Earth-Romulan War human exploration was limited to a small area around the Sol System due to Starfleet's few starships and primitive warp technologies. The *NX* class was the result of the *NX* Project and Zefram Cochrane's Warp Five Project that began prior to his disappearance. The *NX* class was experimental and groundbreaking in nearly every way, including its overall design. Unlike other UESPA and Starfleet vessels of the era, the *NX* class didn't use the cylindrical or box-like hull configurations similar to 20th and 21st century submarines. Instead, the vessel had what would become a standard Starfleet aesthetic: a large saucer-like hull. Further, two long aft-trailing pontoons connected to the class's experimental and powerful warp nacelles. The *NX* class would serve Starfleet for over a decade and was present at some of the most intense battles of the Earth-Romulan War.

CAPABILITIES: Starfleet considered the Warp Five Project a success on the launch of *Enterprise* on April 12th, 2151. The warp core, with significant modifications and with the tendency to use vast amounts of deuterium and antideuterium was able to reach warp 5.06, and during the Earth-Romulan War black-box records indicated that *Atlantis* reached a speed of warp 5.2 in the hours before its destruction. The vessels of the class were heavily armed for a starship of the time as it was thought to err on the side of caution when exploring areas humans had never been before. Three turreted phase cannons were mounted around the saucer to provide excellent coverage against attack from all angles, and six spatial torpedo launchers (four forward and two aft) gave the *NX* class a simulated advantage over possible opponents. The tactical systems were replaced on *Enterprise* in 2153 and installed on subsequent *NX*-class ships, with improved pulsed phase cannons and photonic torpedoes utilizing antimatter in their warheads. Polarized hull-plating and heavy internal bulkheads and structural bracing were used before deflector shield technology was developed. The ship's shuttlebay was located on the ventral surface of the saucer. The two shuttlepods would 'drop' away from the starship when the polarity of the magnetic field of the articulated grappling arm was switched. Debris and small craft that were not under their own propulsion could be brought aboard by two 'grapplers' that could be latched on using both magnets and the servo mounted claws that would grip onto nearly any surface.

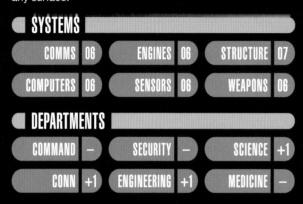

SYSTEMS

COMMS	06	ENGINES	06	STRUCTURE	07
COMPUTERS	06	SENSORS	06	WEAPONS	06

DEPARTMENTS

COMMAND	–	SECURITY	–	SCIENCE	+1
CONN	+1	ENGINEERING	+1	MEDICINE	–

SCALE: 3

ATTACKS:
- Pulse Cannons
- Spatial Torpedoes
- Grappler Cable (Strength 2)

TALENTS
NX-class starships have the following Talents:
- Polarized Hull Plating
- Grappler Cable

CONSTITUTION CLASS REFIT

OVERVIEW: After a detailed proposal from then Lieutenant Commander Montgomery Scott of the U.S.S. *Enterprise* and the San Francisco Shipyards, the decision to perform a 'radical' refit of the *Constitution* class was accepted. Many of the modifications and systems upgrades were specifically requested by Scott due to his experience serving on board the *Enterprise* during its five-year mission under Captain James T. Kirk. The entire exterior of the starship was altered as new hull plating and bulkhead compartments were installed across the ship, and new warp nacelles containing warp coils nearly twice as efficient as the ones previously used. While the *Constitution* class refit would only continue to serve in Starfleet until the late

The following rules apply to Earth Starfleet vessels in the 22nd century:

22ND CENTURY WEAPONS

- **Phase weapons** are energy weapons, like Phasers though less sophisticated. A Phase weapon has the Versatile 1 quality.

- **Spatial Torpedoes** are simple chemical explosive warheads fitted into a guided missile, used by Earth Starfleet vessels in the early 22nd century. They have a Range of Medium, and a base damage of 2⚔, modified by the ship's Security as normal. They have no damage effects or special qualities.

- **Photonic Torpedoes** are a precursor to photon torpedoes, using an antimatter charge under magnetic containment, though the delivery method is still unsophisticated, and they weren't widespread during the Earth-Romulus War. They have a Range of Long, and a base damage of 2⚔ High Yield, modified by the ship's Security as normal.

- **Nuclear Warheads** use a fission or fusion reaction to generate intense heat, radiation, and explosive force. They're crude but effective, and were used extensively during the Earth-Romulus War. Nuclear warheads are torpedoes — the warheads are loaded into conventional Spatial Torpedoes — with a Range of Medium, and a base damage of 3⚔ Vicious 1 with the Calibration quality.

22ND CENTURY TALENTS

The following Talents are available to 22nd century vessels from Earth's Starfleet, such as the *NX* class.

POLARIZED HULL PLATING

The ship does not have deflector shielding, but rather is equipped with layers of hull plating that can be polarized to resist attack. This functions in the same way as Shields do, with one difference: the ship suffers a Breach if four or more damage is suffered after deductions for Resistance.

GRAPPLER CABLES

This precursor to tractor beams uses sturdy cables and magnetic grapplers to grab on to objects and ships. This functions as a tractor beam, but if the target breaks free, roll 1⚔ — on an Effect, the cables have been Damaged and cannot be used again until repaired.

PHOTONIC TORPEDOES

The vessel is equipped with photonic torpedoes instead of spatial torpedoes.

NUCLEAR WARHEADS

The vessel is equipped with nuclear warheads in addition to its spatial torpedoes. This Talent cannot be taken if the ship does not have spatial torpedoes.

2290s, the technology and design elements developed during the refit would be applied across the fleet to nearly every warp capable vessel and still be seen in starships into the late 24th century.

CAPABILITIES: While the cosmetic differences in the ships exterior are at first striking, the differences in ships systems are even more so. Before, the *Constitution* class phaser systems had independent power supplies, but now phaser power was directly tied to the warp core. This gave the phaser an increase strength and rate of fire. The changes in the EPS grid to allow the warp tie-in with the phaser systems, along with larger and more complex sensor equipment, required the ships photon torpedo launcher to be moved out of the primary hull into the connecting 'neck' dorsal above the design's main deflector dish. A new propulsion power distribution system was devised that allowed warp power to be channeled into the impulse core through an impulse deflection system on the dorsal surface of the primary hull just forward of the impulse deck. This gave the design an incredible sublight acceleration potential in emergencies when warp power wasn't needed elsewhere. Interior spaces for the crew were improved with a recreation room and botanical garden in the secondary hull and a more spacious shuttlebay was created by removing unnecessary bulkheads between the old shuttlebay and cargo areas. This gave the *Constitution* class a greater ability to be assigned larger mission specific secondary craft or carry more supplies.

RULES: Any *Constitution*-class vessel in service after 2270 will have undergone the refit. However, the statistics for the vessel do not change in any way except for the normal refits the ship will have, and perhaps the choice of Talents selected for the ship.

HERMES CLASS
ENTERED SERVICE: 2242

Overview: The *Hermes*-class scout was designed in conjunction with the *Constitution* class, the *Saladin* class, and the *Ptolemy* class. Sharing basic design elements and equipment with its sister classes, the *Hermes* class was highly successful. The *Hermes* class shared the same basic saucer-like primary hull and 'neck' dorsal as other vessels, that connected to a single warp nacelle. Internally the design was quite successful in its role as a scout, but the ship's small size and lack of mission adaptable space in its single hull made the *Hermes* class fall out of use by the 2280s. Some demilitarized *Hermes*-class starships were donated to civilian agencies across the Federation and continued to see use as research vessels for universities into the 24th century.

CAPABILITIES: The ship's single warp nacelle created a powerful enough warp field from its two sets of warp coils that the *Hermes* class was able to have a much smaller matter/antimatter warp core than the *Constitution* class, fitting the entire engineering section into the neck and lower portion of the aft saucer. With the two sets of warp coils so close together, the *Hermes* class could maintain a strong field gradient for a minimal amount of power allowing it to maintain high warp velocities for longer. This meant that most commanding officers of a *Hermes*-class vessel could order their vessels to maintain a steady warp 7 and push emergency speeds above warp 9. Sublight propulsion was provided by the standard multistage fusion reactors at the aft of the primary hull. The weapon systems were comprised of only a single phaser bank on the ventral side of the hull, and no photon torpedo systems. The space this makes available in the saucer allows for the addition of extra sensor suites and laboratories networked through the vessel's two large and powerful duotronic computer cores. The *Hermes* class wasn't designed to include a shuttlebay as that space was required for sensor pallets, but it did have three separate docking ports that often carried small travel pods that could be used to move personnel and small amounts of cargo between the starship and orbital facilities and other starships.

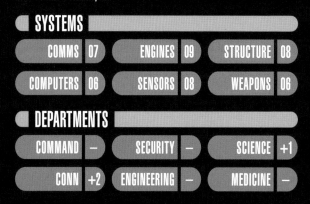

SYSTEMS

COMMS	07	ENGINES	09	STRUCTURE	08
COMPUTERS	06	SENSORS	08	WEAPONS	06

DEPARTMENTS

COMMAND	–	SECURITY	–	SCIENCE	+1
CONN	+2	ENGINEERING	–	MEDICINE	–

SCALE: 4

ATTACKS:
- Phaser Bank
- Tractor Beam (Strength 3)

TALENTS
Hermes-class starships have the following Talents:
- Improved Reaction Control System
- Independent Phaser Supply
- Rugged Design

OBERTH CLASS
ENTERED SERVICE: 2269

OVERVIEW: The design of the *Oberth*–class science vessel comes as a surprise to most who haven't studied the history of Starfleet. The small saucer-like primary hull is home to the approximately 100 crew that served on this ship. Attached directly to the hull were two compact and energy efficient warp nacelles and an engineering deck. The design does have a secondary hull slung below the primary hull connected by two thin pylons that contained the vessels deflector array and extensive sensor systems. The design only saw limited use in Starfleet, as other vessels of the time performed the same functions much more effectively, but its small size and low resource requirements meant that many civilian agencies and universities could utilize the class.

CAPABILITIES: The *Oberth* class utilized highly efficient warp coils allowing the vessel to only carry small amounts of antimatter and allowing more space to be dedicated to sensors and a small shuttlebay at the far forward of the primary hull. These warp coils were powered separately by their own small matter/antimatter reactors, allowing each of the reactors to operate on lower settings to reduce strain on the power systems and to interfere less with sensitive detection devices in the secondary hull. Even at full power, the *Oberth* class was limited to achieving warp 8 for brief periods and could only cruise at warp 5. The secondary hull was inaccessible except through access tubes during normal operation. Inside was the planetary survey and subspace scanning equipment that made the *Oberth* class useful for research. The isolated sensor networks, dedicated duotronic computer core and shielded electronics were mirrored on the port and starboard sides of the hull giving the ship interferometric sensor readings that were more detailed than what most starship systems could provide. The isolation of these sensors was necessary due to their sensitivity and high energy output, and unprotected humanoids could be exposed to high energy EM and subspace radiation while scanning operations were underway. The *Oberth* class was taken out of active service in Starfleet after the introduction of isolinear computer systems that rendered most systems on the design obsolete, but a few of the class can still be seen used by Starfleet Academy as training vessels with their warp cores removed and by universities requiring mobile research vessels.

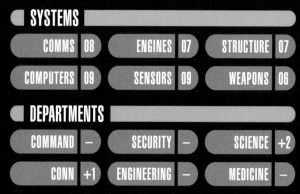

SYSTEMS

COMMS	08	ENGINES	07	STRUCTURE	07
COMPUTERS	09	SENSORS	09	WEAPONS	06

DEPARTMENTS

COMMAND	–	SECURITY	–	SCIENCE	+2
CONN	+1	ENGINEERING	–	MEDICINE	–

SCALE: 3

ATTACKS:
- Phaser Banks
- Tractor Beam (Strength 2)

TALENTS
Oberth-class starships have the following Talents:
- High Resolution Sensors
- Improved Warp Drive

SYDNEY CLASS
ENTERED SERVICE: 2279

OVERVIEW: Colonization efforts across the Federation began to increase in the 2270s and '80s with the introduction of more efficient terraforming techniques and the expansion of the Federation into new sectors, opening dozens of new worlds. A new vessel was designed at the Luna Shipyards in the Sol System that could transport a large group of colonists along with their equipment and supplies. It was dubbed the Sydney-class transport, a boxy, angular, but highly effective starship. In service with Starfleet and multiple civilian agencies beginning in 2279, it would continue to be used until the present day in a multitude of configurations.

CAPABILITIES: The *Sydney*-class was designed specifically to carry as many personnel as possible to a colony as quickly as possible. This meant a compromise between size and speed. The same nacelle and warp coil sets as the *Constitution* and *Miranda*-class starships were utilized along with a powerful warp core allowing the vessel to achieve warp 6. Sublight propulsion was accomplished via a series of impulse reactor ports at the aft and on the ventral surface of the transport. This gave it not only an incredible agility, but also could allow it to land on a planet's surface safely and launch again with its cargo holds full. This class didn't have to land on a planet to deliver its supplies as it had some of the largest transporters developed at the time. These vessels proved to be so useful that many private groups began requesting them as they wished to use them as merchant craft trading goods throughout the quadrants.

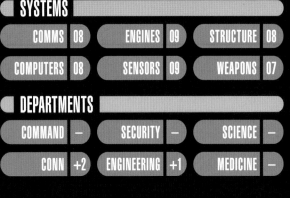

SYSTEMS

COMMS	08	ENGINES	09	STRUCTURE	08
COMPUTERS	08	SENSORS	09	WEAPONS	07

DEPARTMENTS

COMMAND	–	SECURITY	–	SCIENCE	–
CONN	+2	ENGINEERING	+1	MEDICINE	–

SCALE: 4

ATTACKS:
- Tractor Beam (Strength 2)

TALENTS
Sydney-class transports have the following Talents:
- Improved Impulse Drive
- Rugged Design

CENTAUR CLASS
ENTERED SERVICE: 2285

OVERVIEW: In the mid-2280s Starfleet felt that the next generation of light cruisers should begin development based on the new technologies in development for the *Excelsior* class, but the initial failures of the prototype transwarp systems in the *Excelsior* class meant delays for the *Centaur* class. Extensive redesigns of most systems were undertaken by the mid-2290s, with additional vessels of the class beyond the prototype coming into service. Externally this class resembles the *Excelsior* class in many regards including sharing the same saucer for its primary hull and elongated transwarp-style nacelles. The *Centaur* class was only produced in small numbers, not an amount that would allow the retirement of the *Miranda* class.

CAPABILITIES: The first comment from officers first serving onboard *Centaur*-class vessels is always about its speed. The impulse deck of the vessel was designed to move the bulk of an *Excelsior*-class starship nimbly at sublight speeds, but without a secondary hull *Centaur*-class vessels strain the limits of inertial damping fields with their acceleration. They are also over 10% faster at warp velocities when compared to *Excelsior*-class vessels and have a more stable field generated by its widely-spaced nacelles. This speed was utilized primarily for rapid emergency response, making *Centaur*-class vessels the first on the scene during or after an attack on Federation assets or territory. To aid in this task the design included a significant amount of phaser emplacements as well as fore and aft-mounted photon torpedo launchers. A forward-facing shuttlebay could be equipped with a wide variety of small craft and a high-

powered tractor-repulse launch system allowing for high-speed deployment of the auxiliary craft. The *Centaur*-class is seen as a specialist vessel in the 2370s and a few are still in service across the Federation being maintained from utilizing parts from mothballed vessels.

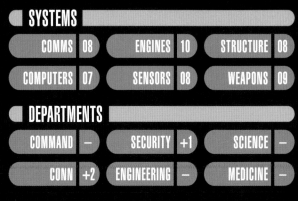

SYSTEMS

COMMS	08	ENGINES	10	STRUCTURE	08
COMPUTERS	07	SENSORS	08	WEAPONS	09

DEPARTMENTS

COMMAND	–	SECURITY	+1	SCIENCE	–
CONN	+2	ENGINEERING	–	MEDICINE	–

SCALE: 4

ATTACKS:
- Phaser Banks
- Photon Torpedoes
- Tractor Beam (Strength 3)

TALENTS
Centaur-class starships have the following Talents.
- Improved Impulse Drive
- Improved Warp Drive

AMBASSADOR CLASS
ENTERED SERVICE: 2335

OVERVIEW: Just after the turn of the 24th century, the Starfleet Exploratory Division and the Federation Science Council began to see a steady decline in scientific returns from deep space missions. By this time Starfleet had been relying on the *Excelsior* class and the few *Constitution*-class starships still in service to continue its aims of discovery, but even with refits, both vessels required frequent returns to starbases. Both organizations asked Utopia Planitia Fleet Yards to develop a new deep-space exploration cruiser that was heavily armed for self-defense, but also capable of staying on assignment for years at a time. The *Ambassador* class was developed and launched in 2335, and many of the engineering techniques, design ideas, and technologies created for this starship would continue to be refined over the coming decades and become the basis for the *Galaxy* class.

CAPABILITIES: The layout of the *Ambassador* class is similar to most Starfleet cruisers, with a saucer-shaped primary hull and a cylindrical secondary engineering hull. The most obvious difference is the then unique warp nacelles that contained high-efficiency warp coils with directional subspace buffers. This meant that subspace distortions and stress could be directed away from weaker coils when they began to show stress. This fine-scale monitoring and field manipulation was only possible with the newly developed FTL isolinear computer cores that the *Ambassador* class was fitted with. Other technological innovations were the first type-9 phaser strips (the precursor to the Galaxy class's type-10 systems), the first fully automated photon torpedo systems on the front and aft of the starship, and the first fully integrated food and equipment replicators aboard a large Starfleet vessel. This class was an immediate success but also a victim of its own innovation. Research and development continued on the groundbreaking systems, improving them faster than they could be installed in the vessels and it quickly became apparent that the *Ambassador* class wasn't able to keep up with technological development, and production was halted on further spaceframes, replacing newer construction with the vastly superior *Galaxy* class.

SYSTEMS

| COMMS | 09 | ENGINES | 09 | STRUCTURE | 10 |
| COMPUTERS | 09 | SENSORS | 09 | WEAPONS | 09 |

DEPARTMENTS

| COMMAND | +1 | SECURITY | – | SCIENCE | +1 |
| CONN | +1 | ENGINEERING | – | MEDICINE | – |

SCALE: 5

ATTACKS:
- Phaser Arrays
- Photon Torpedoes
- Tractor Beam (Strength 4)

TALENTS
Ambassador-class starships have the following Talents:
- High-Resolution Sensors
- Improved Impulse Drive
- Saucer Separation

NEBULA CLASS
ENTERED SERVICE: 2361

OVERVIEW: During the development of the *Galaxy* class, Starfleet felt that they could make the next evolutionary step of the *Miranda* class based on the design elements of the *Galaxy* class, in the same way the *Miranda* had incorporated elements from the refit of the *Constitution* class vessels. The initial design and production contracts were awarded to Yoyodyne Propulsion Systems at the 40 Eridani A Starfleet Construction Yards. Yoyodyne ensured that design elements of the old *Miranda* class that were well respected were included in the new design including modularity of its systems, a large and easily

MISSION POD

Every *Nebula*-class starship is fitted with a single Mission Pod, chosen from the list below. The Talents provided by the pod may not be swapped out normally, but the entire mission pod (and all of its benefits) may be swapped out as if it were a single Talent.

- **Command & Control:** The pod contains additional subspace antennae and supplementary computer cores, allowing it to serve as a command vessel for fleet actions. The ship has +1 Communications, +1 Computers, and +1 Command. The ship also has the Command Ship and Electronic Warfare Systems Talent.

- **Sensors:** The pod contains additional sensor systems, allowing the ship to serve a range of scientific and reconnaissance roles. The ship has +2 Sensors, and +1 Science. The ship also has the Advanced Sensor Suites and High Resolution Sensors Talents.

- **Weapons:** The pod contains additional torpedo launchers, phaser arrays, and targeting sensors. The ship has +1 Sensors, +1 Weapons, and +1 Security. The ship also has the Fast Targeting Systems and Rapid-Fire Torpedo Launcher Talents.

replaceable systems pod on the apex of a 'roll-bar', and interchangeable hull pieces with the *Galaxy*-class under construction at Utopia Planitia.

CAPABILITIES: While heavily based on the layout of the old *Miranda* class, the *Nebula* class differed in its use of an unmodified primary saucer-like hull and the inclusion of a secondary hull that was only slightly modified from the *Galaxy* standard in the first production runs, and unmodified in subsequent runs. This means that *Nebula*-class starships had nearly the same internal volume as the *Galaxy* class. The internal space of the design also differed from the *Galaxy* with more non-modular permanent scientific laboratories, engineering shops, and a fourth computer core (the *Galaxy* class had three) that helped in the transfer of information to and from the equipment pod. The roll-bar mount was much stronger structurally and provided more EPS connections than the *Miranda* class and this allowed a far wider selection of modular pods to be made available for use on the design. The pods that are typically available for the *Nebula* class at major starbases are: sensor array with multispectral and subspace interferometry, a subspace antenna array and repeater, additional matter/antimatter reactor core with two warp nacelles to provide an increased time at high warp speeds, shuttle or fighter launch bay, weapons pod including two type-10 phaser strips and six photon torpedo launchers, or a dedicated photon torpedo deck with sixteen individual launch systems.

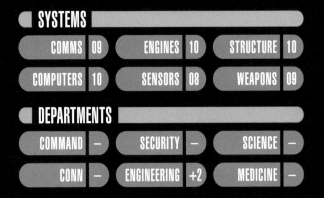

SYSTEMS

COMMS	09	ENGINES	10	STRUCTURE	10
COMPUTERS	10	SENSORS	08	WEAPONS	09

DEPARTMENTS

COMMAND	–	SECURITY	–	SCIENCE	–
CONN	–	ENGINEERING	+2	MEDICINE	–

SCALE: 5

ATTACKS:
- Phaser Arrays
- Photon Torpedoes
- Tractor Beam (Strength 4)

TALENTS

Nebula-class starships have the two Talents determined by the type of mission pod equipped (above), plus the following Talent:
- Saucer Separation

NEW ORLEANS CLASS
ENTERED SERVICE: 2364

OVERVIEW: Soon after the development of the *Galaxy* and *Nebula*-class starships, Starfleet saw the new design style as innovative, but requiring large amounts of resources for each of the ships to be constructed. Starfleet Command issued directives to shipyards across the Federation to design and produce starships for various mission profiles using the same design elements of their newest vessels, but keeping the crew sizes smaller than the *Galaxy* and *Nebula* classes. The *New Orleans*-class heavy frigate was the first design submitted for approval by the San Francisco Fleet Yards. This ship was considerably more compact than most vessels in service at the time, and its non-modular primary and secondary hulls made construction easier and took nearly quarter the time to build compared to a *Nebula* class. The *New Orleans* class has begun to replace *Miranda*-class vessels in active service, but construction rates imply that this full change over won't finish until 2377.

CAPABILITIES: The *New Orleans* class is primarily assigned to patrol and planetary survey missions, similar to the *Miranda* class. The design has two main features that make it highly desired for these missions: a mission adaptable pod on its ventral secondary hull, and two interlinked subspace and EM sensor strips down the side of its secondary hull and along its warp nacelles. The mission pod closely resembles the two photon torpedo / probe launch systems on its dorsal primary hull, but It contains its own isolinear computer core and as many planetary sensors as a *Galaxy*-

class ship typically carries. In addition, this planetary survey pod contains six fully automated remote sample probes that can enter a planet's atmosphere and return biological and geological samples to isolation chambers that are physically separate from the rest of the vessel, making contamination highly unlikely. The two subspace sensor arrays along the hull and the warp nacelles allow long-range and highly detailed sensor scans on star systems dozens of parsecs away through interferometry. These same sensor networks allow the *New Orleans* class the ability to have a detailed map of subspace fluctuations and turbulence around it, allowing its warp coils to tweak power output in such a way that it mimics the variable warp geometry of an *Intrepid*-class starship without the adjustable-pitch warp pylons.

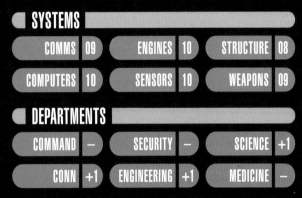

SYSTEMS

COMMS	09	ENGINES	10	STRUCTURE	08
COMPUTERS	10	SENSORS	10	WEAPONS	09

DEPARTMENTS

COMMAND	–	SECURITY	–	SCIENCE	+1
CONN	+1	ENGINEERING	+1	MEDICINE	–

SCALE: 4

ATTACKS:
- Phaser Arrays
- Photon Torpedoes
- Tractor Beam (Strength 3)

TALENTS

New Orleans-class starships have the following Talents:
- High Resolution Sensors
- Modular Laboratories

OLYMPIC CLASS
ENTERED SERVICE: 2368

OVERVIEW: Starfleet had been relying on its exploration vessels as hospital ships since soon after the Earth-Romulan War. Starfleet felt that a dedicated hospital ship was a waste of highly trained medical personnel that could be assigned across the fleet otherwise. A change in this perspective began in the late 2360s with disastrous encounters with the Borg and increased tensions with the Cardassians and other aggressive interstellar governments. It was also seen that a vessel that was a non-combatant and solely used for humanitarian efforts could help diplomatically with neutral systems that were wavering between joining the Federation or other political entities. The *Olympic* class began limited production at various shipyards across the Federation in 2368, and while few are currently in service, they have made an impact.

CAPABILITIES: The *Olympic* class was designed to look like no other Starfleet vessel currently in service, only resembling the starships used during the Earth-Romulan War such as the *Daedalus* class with a large spherical primary hull and an angular secondary hull. This was to make the starship unable to be confused with other Starfleet vessels so it would better stand out as a non-combatant in warzones. The primary hull contained the crew quarters, main computer, and command systems, as well as a sizable botanical garden filled with medicinal plants from across the Federation and beyond. To help with identification, the logo of Starfleet Medical is displayed prominently on each side of the primary hull. The main sickbay used for the crew was also located in the primary hull, but the hospital complex was located in the secondary hull. This hospital complex could house, isolate, and treat over 500 humanoids requiring intensive care and the crew could quickly adapt other spaces inside the ship to house another 500 in triage situations. Newly built *Olympic*-class ships are also being fitted with the Emergency Medical Hologram system. While the *Olympic* class is considered a non-combatant, Starfleet insisted that a 'minimum amount of defensive weaponry' be installed, so low power type-8 Phaser arrays circle the outer primary hull, barely powerful enough to rattle a starship, but enough to destroy incoming debris, or cut away sections of starship hull to have rescue teams reach trapped personnel. The design contains a sizeable shuttlebay that is typically equipped with runabouts and larger shuttles to be used for personnel evacuations or medical supply shipments.

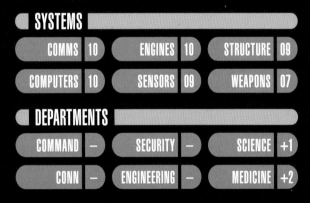

SYSTEMS

COMMS	10	ENGINES	10	STRUCTURE	09
COMPUTERS	10	SENSORS	09	WEAPONS	07

DEPARTMENTS

COMMAND	–	SECURITY	–	SCIENCE	+1
CONN	–	ENGINEERING	–	MEDICINE	+2

SCALE: 4

ATTACKS:
- Phaser Arrays
- Tractor Beam (Strength 3)

TALENTS
Olympic-class starships have the following Talents:
- Advanced Sickbay
- Modular Laboratories
- Dedicated Personnel (Medical)

STEAMRUNNER CLASS
ENTERED SERVICE: 2370

OVERVIEW: Light and fast, the *Steamrunner* class filled multiple roles in Starfleet including light escort, interceptor, electronic warfare, and surveillance/intelligence. The design consists of an angular saucer for a primary hull containing all vital systems, and a detached secondary hull that is suspended between the starship's two warp nacelles. During shakedown cruises, new crew quickly discovered that the densely-packed systems could cause interference between the warp nacelles, the deflector system, and long-range sensors, but they quickly learned how to tweak the systems to perform at peak efficiency.

CAPABILITIES: The primary role of the *Steamrunner* class was intelligence gathering and surveillance. This meant that sensor systems were given a high priority in allocation of the internal space. The number of EM and subspace scanning devices requires the use of three separate computer cores, two of which are in the main saucer and a single core in the detached secondary hull. This aft computer not only deals with incoming data from aft sensors and the deflector array, but also controls the electronic warfare systems, transporter systems, and the warp field stabilizer that allows the *Steamrunner* class to maintain high warp speeds for longer durations. The small size of the vessel meant that the warp core installed had to be compact, and the power output had to be carefully monitored and adjusted, allowing the sensor and electronic warfare systems to operate at the expense of sub-space field generation from the warp nacelles. In practice this meant that while the starship was at warp the EW systems and long-range sensors had limited ranges, but at sub-light speeds *Steamrunner* sensors and EW systems could operate at extreme ranges, exceeding those on most Starfleet designs. The sensors can accurately detect starships and even shuttlecraft-sized objects ranging out to a distance of several parsecs and have enough resolution to monitor technological civilizations the Federation is considering making first contact with at those same ranges. These same sensors make it a superb stellar surveyor and planetary mapper, and *Steamrunner*-class vessels have also become well regarded as medium-range exploration craft.

SYSTEMS

COMMS	10	ENGINES	11	STRUCTURE	09
COMPUTERS	09	SENSORS	10	WEAPONS	10

DEPARTMENTS

COMMAND	–	SECURITY	+1	SCIENCE	+1
CONN	+1	ENGINEERING	–	MEDICINE	–

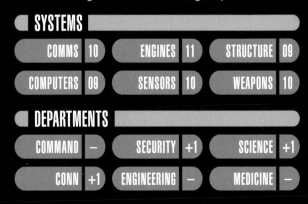

SCALE: 4

WEAPONRY
- Phaser Arrays
- Photon Torpedoes
- Tractor Beam (Strength 3)

TALENTS
Steamrunner-class starships have the following Talents:
- Advanced Sensor Suites
- Improved Warp Drive

NORWAY CLASS
ENTERED SERVICE: 2371

OVERVIEW: The Advanced Starship Design Bureau at Earth Spacedock designs and produces prototypes every year for Starfleet to consider for active service. One area they saw Starfleet lacking in was rapid emergency responders. Design and production of the *Norway*-class starship began in 2369. ASDB gave its design a compact wedge-shaped hull with the engineering section located in the aft portion of the ship. The first two vessels of the class were launched in early 2371, *U.S.S. Norway* and *U.S.S. Finland*. Both

have already responded to emergencies in the core of the Federation and Starfleet has ordered more production runs of this design to be assigned to other dense areas of inhabited worlds.

CAPABILITIES: As an emergency response vessel, the *Norway* class has extensive personnel transporters, expanded sickbay and biological science facilities to handle wounded and to research viral and bacterial infections that often cause pain and suffering. Also, the design includes a shuttlebay capable of handling two Type-6 shuttlecraft in a 'ready launch' set up and a shuttle elevator provides access to the shuttle maintenance bay that typically holds at least two other shuttles of various models, one of which being a Type 7 often loaded with emergency food and medical supplies ready to be delivered to a stricken starship or planet's surface. Large cargo bays on the dorsal section of the starship allow significant amounts of material to be brought to a needed area, but the ASDB also included two tractor beam emitters above the shuttle launch bay that allow small cargo containers to be towed between the vessels warp nacelles while under power in case internal cargo bays aren't adequate. This ship could normally cruise at warp 7 and achieve short bursts of warp 9.7, but with tractored cargo interfering with the vessel's warp field, maximum sustained speeds were lowered to warp 6.5 with short bursts of warp 9.2. As a relief ship, it was assumed the *Norway* class would be entering war zones, so the design includes defensive shielding 5% stronger than starships of similar mass and includes secondary shield generators for the warp core and bridge. The design also includes multiple type-10 phaser strips and both a forward and rear-mounted torpedo launcher.

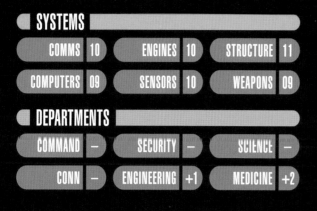

SYSTEMS

COMMS	10	ENGINES	10	STRUCTURE	11
COMPUTERS	09	SENSORS	10	WEAPONS	09

DEPARTMENTS

COMMAND	–	SECURITY	–	SCIENCE	–
CONN	–	ENGINEERING	+1	MEDICINE	+2

SCALE: 4

ATTACKS:

- Phaser Arrays
- Photon Torpedoes
- Tractor Beam (Strength 3)

TALENTS

Norway-class starships have the following Talents:

- Advanced Sickbay
- Emergency Medial Hologram

SABER CLASS
ENTERED SERVICE: 2371

OVERVIEW: Patrolling the outer reaches of the Federation has always been a problem. During the rapid expansion of the Federation in the early 24th century, this became a larger problem as the volume of space needing patrols and assignments requiring escort of essential goods grew exponentially. This duty originally fell to any Starfleet vessel in the area to be called on to help in emergencies such as attacks on interstellar commercial vessels or other crimes. Starfleet felt the need to design and produce a patrol vessel dedicated to maintaining a presence on the edges of Federation space to better respond to raiders and piracy, but also be able to perform basic survey duties. This hybrid vessel was the *Saber* class.

CAPABILITIES: Small and compact, the *Saber* class has an angular primary hull with an integrated engineering section at its aft. The forward section of the primary hull has a cut-

out that contains two large shuttlebay doors leading inside a spacious launch and maintenance bay for the vessel's four shuttlecraft, typically two Type-6 and two Type-9, with two of the shuttles maintained in a 'Ready' launch condition. In some cases these vessels also include two Work Bee maintenance pods, but this can make maneuvering the shuttles inside the bay more difficult and few crews keep them on board for long. As a patrol vessel, the *Saber* class has sensors specifically dedicated to detection of warp signatures and neutrinos from fusion reactors, allowing easy detection of starships and other spacecraft. The design also includes powerful tractor beams linked directly into the warp power system, capable of towing vessels much larger than it and even halting those same starships under full impulse power. To help stop fleeing criminals, these ships also include powerful impulse drives on the aft with vectored magnetic flow mounts as well as extensive RCS systems across the rest of the vessel, providing heavy thrust in any direction needed to counter the thrust of an escaping vessel. As Starfleet wished the ship to also double as a survey vessel, all *Saber*-class vessels have an extensive sensor suite that is particularly suited to detecting spatial and planetary anomalies, but unsuitable for larger bodies as the size of the starship limits the power and number of planetary sensors able to provide deep geological scans from orbit. Currently Starfleet has plans to have at least one of this class assigned to each border sector, but deployment has been limited to the Romulan border area nearest Earth due to production of the design just beginning.

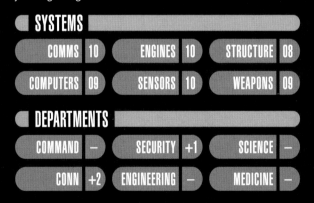

SYSTEMS

COMMS	10	ENGINES	10	STRUCTURE	08
COMPUTERS	09	SENSORS	10	WEAPONS	09

DEPARTMENTS

COMMAND	–	SECURITY	+1	SCIENCE	–
CONN	+2	ENGINEERING	–	MEDICINE	–

SCALE: 3

ATTACKS:
- Phaser Arrays
- Photon Torpedoes
- Tractor Beam (Strength 4; effects of High-Power Tractor Beam included)

TALENTS
Saber-class starships have the following Talents:
- High-Power Tractor Beam
- Improved Impulse Drive

SOVEREIGN CLASS
ENTERED SERVICE: 2371

OVERVIEW: The success of the *Galaxy*-class starship wasn't lost on Starfleet or the Federation as a whole. While there were notable losses of the class, the large size and survivability of the class made them influential on starship designers already hard at work building the next major Federation explorer. The *Sovereign* class began development in 2368 after Starfleet Command felt that starships probing deep space would need to be better equipped to handle hostile and more technologically advanced races such as the Borg. The new design gained greater importance after the discovery of the Bajoran wormhole in 2369 and the discovery of damage to space-time caused by standard warp drive systems. The first of the new vessels, *U.S.S. Sovereign* NX/NCC-73811, is expected to enter full service in late 2371.

CAPABILITIES: The *Sovereign* class uses a new variable geometry warp drive able to replicate the same qualities of the Intrepid class's variable pitch warp nacelles without the adjustable pylons. This advanced warp drive is only possible with small, but highly specialized isolinear systems located in each nacelle, able to coordinate the movement of the warp coils inside the nacelle and their emissions through multiple subspace frequencies. The result is the *Sovereign* class does no detectable damage to space-time and can enter warp speeds faster than ships a tenth of its mass. Like the *Galaxy* class before it, the *Sovereign* class has extensive laboratories, sensor systems, and subspace transmitters that make it an excellent deep-space explorer. The vessel has two shuttle bays, one on the primary hull that is the main shuttle bay, and a second shuttle launch and recovery system on the far aft of the engineering hull. A large captain's yacht is also included in the design and is made more functional as an auxiliary vehicle with the inclusion of a small matter/antimatter power core and two warp nacelles. Diplomatic receptions can be held on a planet's surface inside the captain's yacht or onboard the starship with its expansive diplomatic facilities. Command and control systems are integrated into the design's communications systems, allowing the *Sovereign* class to act as a flagship for fleet deployments. The design includes significant firepower including a dedicated quantum torpedo launcher and multiple type-10a phaser strips allowing both offensive and defensive fire modes. The *Sovereign* class doesn't include civilian facilities in the same way as its predecessor class, the *Galaxy*, but still contains many of the features crews previously serving on the *Galaxy* class have grown accustomed to, including a lounge, extensive holodeck simulators, gymnasiums, and even a small kitchen for the crew to cook, as many personnel prefer handmade nourishment to replicated rations.

SYSTEMS

COMMS	09	ENGINES	11	STRUCTURE	10
COMPUTERS	11	SENSORS	09	WEAPONS	10

DEPARTMENTS

COMMAND	+1	SECURITY	+1	SCIENCE	+1
CONN	–	ENGINEERING	–	MEDICINE	–

SCALE: 6

ATTACKS:

- Phaser Arrays
- Photon Torpedoes
- Quantum Torpedoes
- Tractor Beam (Strength 5)

TALENTS

Sovereign-class starships have the following Talents:

- Command Ship
- Emergency Medical Hologram
- Improved Warp Drive
- Quantum Torpedoes

LUNA CLASS

ENTERED SERVICE: 2372 (PROJECTED)

OVERVIEW: With the design success of the *Intrepid* class, Starfleet immediately began a parallel development of a heavy explorer capable of all the same exploratory and scientific assignments of an *Intrepid* class, but with larger research facilities, more computer processing power, and longer mission duration. The *Luna* class exited its design phase eight months after her sister class, and while there have been engineering delays, *U.S.S. Luna* NX-80101 is expected to slip her drydock over Mars in late 2372. Like the *Intrepid* class, the *Luna* class has an integrated primary and secondary engineering hull with organic curves giving it a similar profile to many of the newer Starfleet vessels leaving Utopia Planitia.

CAPABILITIES: Like her sister class, the *Luna* class is equipped with variable geometry warp nacelles, allowing the starship to maintain warp field stability in turbulent space-time and to generate the subspace field with less power. This allows the *Luna* class a cruising speed of Warp 7 and a maximum speed of Warp 9.975. Also like the *Intrepid* class, these vessels are designed to incorporate holo-emitters in sickbay to facilitate an Emergency Medical Hologram, but these emitters are also installed in mission critical areas of the ship. Large sections of the primary hull have areas that allow for modular mission specific research facilities that have hardwired connections into the ships main computer arrays, as well as facilities to allow for non-Class-M environments for studying newly discovered life forms or for hosting non-humanoid sentient species for diplomatic events, and mounts for extra sensor equipment. Unlike its sister class, the *Luna* class has a modular equipment pod much like the *Nebula* class. This pod is typically filled with sensitive subspace and multispectral sensor equipment and a third isolinear computer core that assists the two primary cores. The only pod so far in development is a subspace transceiver that would allow near real-time communications back to Starfleet from distances of up to 50,000 light-years, but this technology is not believed to be ready until after the performance analysis of MIDAS (Mutara Interdimensional Deep Space Array System) is complete once construction is finished.

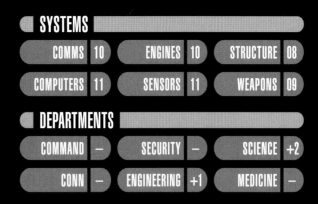

SYSTEMS

| COMMS 10 | ENGINES 10 | STRUCTURE 08 |
| COMPUTERS 11 | SENSORS 11 | WEAPONS 09 |

DEPARTMENTS

| COMMAND — | SECURITY — | SCIENCE +2 |
| CONN — | ENGINEERING +1 | MEDICINE — |

SCALE: 5

ATTACKS:
- Phaser Arrays
- Photon Torpedoes
- Tractor Beam (Strength 4)

TALENTS

Luna-class starships have the following Talents:
- Advanced Research Facilities
- Advanced Sensor Suites
- Emergency Medical Hologram

ADDITIONAL TALENTS

The following Talents may be selected for any starship in this book, and starships from other books in the *Star Trek Adventures* range.

CAPTAIN'S YACHT

The vessel has a single additional support craft, normally mounted in a dedicated port under the saucer section of the ship. These craft, larger than most shuttles, are often used for diplomatic missions and special excursions by the commanding officer, and are often known as the Captain's Yacht (though not always; some Intrepid-class vessels have a similar craft called an aeroshuttle). The ship has one additional Small Craft, which does not count against the number which may be active at any one time, and has the following stats.

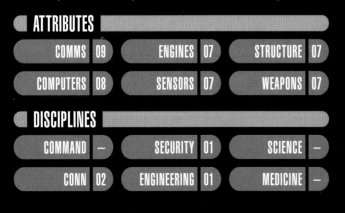

ATTRIBUTES

| COMMS 09 | ENGINES 07 | STRUCTURE 07 |
| COMPUTERS 08 | SENSORS 07 | WEAPONS 07 |

DISCIPLINES

| COMMAND — | SECURITY 01 | SCIENCE — |
| CONN 02 | ENGINEERING 01 | MEDICINE — |

POWER: 4   **SCALE:** 2
SHIELDS: 4   **RESISTANCE:** 2

CREW COMPLEMENT: 1 to 4

ATTACKS:
- Phaser Bank (Energy, Range Medium, 4▲, Versatile 2)
- Micro-torpedoes (Torpedo, Range Long, 4▲ High Yield)

DEDICATED PERSONNEL

Choose a single department. The ship gains two additional Crew Support, which may only be used to establish Supporting Characters who are part of that department.

HIGH-POWER TRACTOR BEAM

The ship's tractor beam systems channel far greater quantities of power and exert much more force on the target. The ship's tractor beam has a strength two higher than normal. Further, the ship may spend Power whenever a target attempts to escape the tractor beam to increase its strength for that attempt; the strength increases by 1 for every two Power spent.

INDEPENDENT PHASER SUPPLY

Common prior to the 2270s, the ship's phasers use an independent power supply, rather than drawing directly from the ship's other power sources. Attacking with the ship's phasers no longer has a Power Requirement. However, the ship may not spend additional Power to boost the effectiveness of an attack with the phasers.

CHAPTER 04.20

FEDERATION VESSELS
FEDERATION SMALL CRAFT

TAKE A SHUTTLE

Shuttlecraft and other small space capable vehicles are commonplace across the Federation in the same way cars and aircraft are on 20th and 21st century Earth. Characters should be familiar with shuttles of all kinds, even from before they joined Starfleet. During Academy training most characters will have gained even more understanding and experience with shuttles, and it's a rare character serving on a starship who would be unable to at least pilot a shuttlecraft from its launch bay to the surface of a world.

TYPE-F SHUTTLE
ENTERED SERVICE: 2255

OVERVIEW: The Type-F "Federation" shuttlecraft was the first fully standardized shuttlecraft manufactured by all shipyards and member worlds. The boxy, but functional design was at first decried by more aesthetically minded Starfleet officers and crew, but the design quickly gained a reputation for reliability, survivability, and versatility not seen in previous Starfleet shuttles. It would be used in its original specifications until the 2280s when it underwent an extensive redesign and refit program, making them continue to resemble Starfleet's design aesthetic and increasing its usefulness.

CAPABILITIES: The squat, angular, and non-aerodynamic form of the Type-F shuttle hides the fact that it had the greatest mass-to-power ratio for any shuttlecraft yet produced. Powered by a tiny matter/antimatter fuel cell in each of its nacelles, the Type F could use its ion-based impulse drive to maintain sublight accelerations equivalent to most starships of its era. These ion impulse drives were so efficient that while in an atmosphere, under normal operating conditions, the Type-F shuttlecraft would act as a ramjet and maintain hypersonic speeds nearly indefinitely. In a vacuum, it was less efficient and would require refueling of reaction mass and its fuel cells every three standard weeks. The Type F was designed to not only provide transport for goods, but also personnel. The maximum normal compliment was seven humanoids, but used as a lifeboat or a troop transport, it could hold nearly double that in cramped conditions for short periods of time. It also had very limited warp capability, making it suited for planetary

survey missions. To assist in this, the shuttle had a powerful duotronic computer system and advanced sensors that could provide extra information to its parent craft. The Type-F shuttle can still be seen in use by Starfleet Academy during atmospheric flight training exercises and formation flying above Paris for the annual United Earth's "Federation Day" Air and Space show.

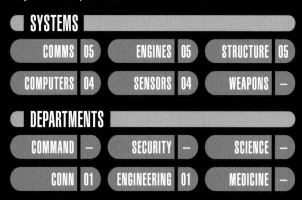

SYSTEMS

| COMMS | 05 | ENGINES | 05 | STRUCTURE | 05 |
| COMPUTERS | 04 | SENSORS | 04 | WEAPONS | – |

DEPARTMENTS

| COMMAND | – | SECURITY | – | SCIENCE | – |
| CONN | 01 | ENGINEERING | 01 | MEDICINE | – |

POWER: 3   **SCALE:** 1
SHIELDS: 2   **RESISTANCE:** 1

CREW COMPLEMENT: 1 or 2, plus 6 passengers

ATTACKS: None.

SPECIAL RULES:
- Rugged Design (Talent)

WORK BEE

ENTERED SERVICE: 2270

OVERVIEW: Small, agile, and made for ease of use, the Cargo Management Unit (CMU), also known as the Work Bee, was introduced in the 2270s and continues to see use across the Federation one hundred years later. The Work Bee's cautionary yellow hull markings resemble Earth honey bees, busy and productive, giving them their nickname.

CAPABILITIES: The Work Bee is very small, barely larger than the humanoid piloting it. The CMU design is so small that users don environmental suits that provide them with a breathable environment as there is no room for a dedicated life-support system. All Work Bees have standard equipment such as a powerful spotlight on the forward hull to illuminate areas of interest and large transparent-aluminum windows allowing the pilot easy viewing of what is often tight spaces around them. Depending on the specific assignment, Work Bees can be outfitted with numerous tools on modular mounts on the fore and aft of the vehicle including cargo hardpoints for hauling small cargo pods, manipulator arms for moving and placing pieces of equipment, welding and cutting torches, inspection scanning devices for checking newly finished construction, and a tool box filled with engineering tools designed to be used by crews in EVA suits. The Work Bee is powered by tiny electro-chemical fuel cells and moves via helium RCS thrusters. Typically Work Bees must replace the RCS and fuel cells after only a few hours of operation making these vehicles closely tied to the facility or starship they call home.

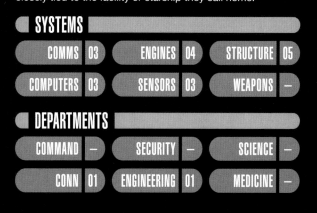

SYSTEMS

COMMS 03	ENGINES 04	STRUCTURE 05
COMPUTERS 03	SENSORS 03	WEAPONS —

DEPARTMENTS

COMMAND —	SECURITY —	SCIENCE —
CONN 01	ENGINEERING 01	MEDICINE —

POWER: 2   **SCALE:** 1
SHIELDS: 2   **RESISTANCE:** 1

CREW COMPLEMENT: 1

ATTACKS: None.

TALENT: None

SPECIAL RULES:
- Cannot use any Helm action other than Maneuver. Provides no life support. Grants an Advantage — "Work Bee Tools" — on all Tasks made to use the Work Bee to perform external repairs on the ship.

TYPE-6 SHUTTLE

ENTERED SERVICE: 2356

OVERVIEW: By the early 2300s, Starfleet knew that the Type-F shuttlecraft was approaching the end of the design's usefulness. The Type-6 shuttlecraft was designed to closely resemble the refitted Type-F shuttle of the 2280s so recovery systems and shuttle platforms wouldn't have to be redesigned across the Federation. An easy to understand and maintain design was required as this shuttle would become the new standard across the Federation.

CAPABILITIES: The Type-6 shuttlecraft was an improvement in design over the Type F with many of its systems. Propulsion systems were upgraded; the impulse drive having its own fusion power core, and the nacelles on the ventral sides of the shuttle actually having warp coils that are powered by their own fusion reactors, giving the shuttle a limited FTL capability of just over warp 1. This speed meant that the shuttle could range further from its parent craft for assignments; it usually wouldn't venture further than a few AUs. The fact that the Type-6 could enter warp meant that the shuttlecraft became ubiquitous as interplanetary transport, making travel between worlds and facilities in a star system nearly five times faster. Improvements in offensive and defensive technologies included the installation of deflector shield emitters, allowing it to survive in more hostile environmental conditions and the addition of two modular type-4 phaser mounts. The addition of extra energy capacitors and power generation for these weapons also gave the Type-6 a higher warp speed, almost reaching warp 2. These shuttlecraft can be found assigned to nearly every Starfleet starbase and ground facilities across the Federation as well as most starships with shuttlebays large enough to hold them.

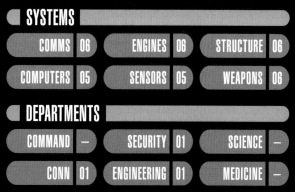

SYSTEMS

COMMS 06	ENGINES 06	STRUCTURE 06
COMPUTERS 05	SENSORS 05	WEAPONS 06

DEPARTMENTS

COMMAND —	SECURITY 01	SCIENCE —
CONN 01	ENGINEERING 01	MEDICINE —

POWER: 3   **SCALE:** 1
SHIELDS: 3   **RESISTANCE:** 1

CREW COMPLEMENT: 1 or 2, plus 6 passengers

ATTACKS:
- Escalation 2 Type-4 Phaser Banks (Range Medium, 3⚠, Versatile 2)

SPECIAL RULES:
- Rugged Design (Talent)

TYPE-7 SHUTTLE
ENTERED SERVICE: 2359

OVERVIEW: Seeing a need for a larger personnel and cargo transport shuttle after the limitations of the internal space of the Type-6 shuttlecraft became apparent, Starfleet issued a directive calling for the design and construction of a larger 'Medium Range Cargo and Personnel Shuttle'. The design that came out on top was from the Baikonur Cosmodrome and was designated the 'Type-7'. The Type-7 was still the box-like shape and two nacelles common to all Starfleet shuttles, but in a deviation from what was expected, its edges were rounded and curved, giving it a fluid shape akin to a sea creature or a tear drop.

CAPABILITIES: Built with the same isolinear computer systems as was standard on the later models of the Type-6, the Type-7 shuttle used a 100 millicochrane field around its computer core to help monitor and adjust its low-power warp field. This heavy computer control was needed to keep the shuttle at superluminal velocities topping out at Warp 2.5. Without the computer assistance, a rookie pilot could easily cause the shuttle to drop to sublight speeds. The interior of the shuttle was large, capable of seating a minimum of two pilots and over ten passengers in comfort, triple that for short duration flights in emergency situations. Nearly all the shuttle's power was needed for propulsion, leaving little for deflector shields, and none for weapon systems. This lack of adequate defenses meant that starships operating away from Federation space rarely used the Type-7, they were usually assigned to starbases and star systems inside Federation territory.

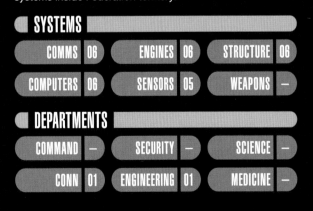

SYSTEMS

COMMS	06	ENGINES	06	STRUCTURE	06
COMPUTERS	06	SENSORS	05	WEAPONS	—

DEPARTMENTS

COMMAND	—	SECURITY	—	SCIENCE	—
CONN	01	ENGINEERING	01	MEDICINE	—

POWER: 3   **SCALE:** 1
SHIELDS: 3   **RESISTANCE:** 1

CREW COMPLEMENT: 1 or 2, plus 12 passengers

ATTACKS: None.

SPECIAL RULES:

- **Well-Supplied:** A Type-7 shuttle is well-supplied and contains many storage compartments. Characters may attempt to search the shuttle for parts or supplies by attempting an Insight + Engineering Task with a Difficulty of 2. The Gamemaster determines what these supplies or parts do, based on what the characters are attempting to find.
- **Unstable Warp Field:** A character operating a Type-7 shuttle increases the Difficulty of any Task to go to warp by 1.

TYPE-8 SHUTTLE
ENTERED SERVICE: 2371

OVERVIEW: The introduction of the *Sovereign*, *Intrepid*, and *Nova*-class starships meant that design teams had the chance to rework and update the reliable Type-6 shuttlecraft. The Type-8 was the result, visually almost identical to the Type-6 and able to use the same maintenance facilities and docking ports as the older model.

CAPABILITIES: The major difference in standard systems in the Type-8 over the Type-6 was a more compact and powerful matter/antimatter warp core. Inset bussard collectors in the port and starboard intakes were larger enough that the shuttlecraft only carried small deuterium tanks compared to its larger antimatter storage cells. This extra power gave the Type-8 a higher sustained warp speed of 2.8. The shuttle was capable of warp 3.1, but only for short durations before the warp coils drained the field capacitors and forced the shuttle to spend hours at sublight speeds recharging its systems. Like the Type-6, the Type-8 had the option of mounting two phasers on the nose of the vessel, requiring one of the shuttle pilots to be tactically trained. The use of the phasers would also put a strain on the shuttle's warp systems, and firing the phasers in a tactical situation often meant forgoing the possibility of going to warp soon after.

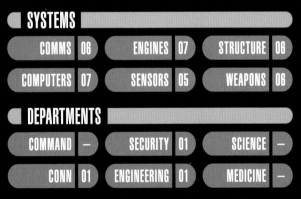

SYSTEMS

COMMS	06	ENGINES	07	STRUCTURE	06
COMPUTERS	07	SENSORS	05	WEAPONS	06

DEPARTMENTS

COMMAND	—	SECURITY	01	SCIENCE	—
CONN	01	ENGINEERING	01	MEDICINE	—

POWER: 3   **SCALE:** 1
SHIELDS: 3   **RESISTANCE:** 1

CREW COMPLEMENT: 1 or 2, plus 6 passengers

ATTACKS: Escalation 2 Phaser Bank (Range Medium, 3▲, Versatile 2)

SPECIAL RULES:

- Rugged Design (Talent)

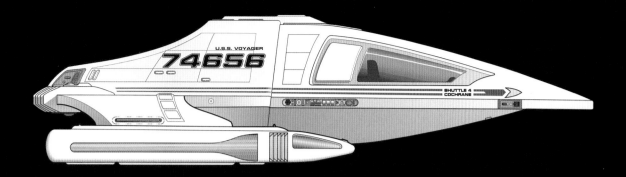

TYPE-9 SHUTTLE
ENTERED SERVICE: 2370

OVERVIEW: The Type-9 shuttlecraft was also referred to as the Class 2 (second-class) after the Type-8 shuttlecraft was given priority in production over the arguably more elegant and smaller Type-9. The Type-9 was originally designed as a single crew warp-capable fighter to replace the larger multi-crewed fighters currently deployed in defensive formations across the Federation, but initial flight tests showed that the design would be far more successful as a small shuttlecraft with its internal space dedicated to sensors and cargo rather than shielding and offensive systems.

CAPABILITIES: As holdovers from its initial role as a fighter, the Type-9 has incredible agility at sublight speeds. This maneuverability also extends into superluminal speeds with the Type-9 able to reduce power in a single nacelle to as low as 5% of its maximum energy rating, putting heavy torque on the subspace field and giving it warp maneuverability and stability that is unrivalled. Also as a holdover, the Type-9 has a permanently installed phaser system in its forward section and can be retrofitted with a limited use ventral mounted photon torpedo launcher. While its offensive systems are more than most shuttlecraft, its defensive systems are lacking. Sustained fire from a handheld type-3 phaser rifle can overwhelm the shields and knock them out, so use in hostile environments is out of the question. The sensors systems once used to target and analyze hostile vessels make the Type-9 successful as a secondary exploration vehicle. Mounts for tachyon transmitters and receivers are also located on the outside of the shuttle, allowing them to network with other vessels to form a tachyon detection grid to use against Dominion, Klingon, or Romulan cloaking devices.

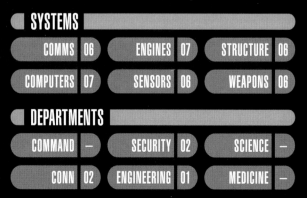

POWER: 4   **SCALE:** 1
SHIELDS: 4   **RESISTANCE:** 1

CREW COMPLEMENT: 1, plus 2 passengers

ATTACKS:
- Phaser Bank (Range Medium, 5▲, Versatile 2).
- **Escalation 2** Photon Torpedoes (Torpedo, Range Long, 4▲ High Yield)

SPECIAL RULES:
- Improved Impulse Drive (Talent)

TYPE-10 SHUTTLE
ENTERED SERVICE: 2370

OVERVIEW: With the new smaller starships beginning to be put into production by Starfleet, compact shuttles were needed to give these vessels the versatility expected by the officers and enlisted of the service. To accomplish this, designers had to make compromises in the design, electing for compact systems rather than the best available for Federation shuttles. The Type-10 shuttlecraft, also known as the *Chaffee* class, ended up using technology that had been discarded for a century or more as refinements to the equipment made them small enough to be required for this design. Loved and hated in equal measures by crew serving aboard them, the Type-10 is only permanently assigned to *Defiant* and some *Nova*-class starships.

CAPABILITIES: The Type-10 can handle up to four crew (and double that number in emergencies), but typically only has a crew of two assigned for away missions. This interior space is surprising for such a small shuttle. The openness of the Type-10 is only made possible due to the shuttle's reliance on compact fusion reactors in its two engine pods for power. Without a bulky matter/antimatter reactor, more of these small reactors, along with more capacitors allow the Type-10 to maintain a cruising speed of Warp 3 and a burst speed of Warp 5 that can be sustained for approximately thirty seconds. As the Type-10 is typically assigned to combat vessels or small and under-armed science vessels, it has three hard-mounted type-5 phaser strips, one on each engine pod and one on the nose of the shuttle. The Type-10 also has a hardpoint on its ventral surface that allows the mounting of a micro-torpedo launcher for a single-shot quantum torpedo. Crews often complained about how many systems were located outside on the engine pods. As EVA suits are not standard on the Type-10 due to their bulk, damage to propulsion systems and hull damage were very difficult to repair. This isn't typically an issue as reports of reactor damage to the Type-10 results in high-energy plasma burning through the entire engine pod, and damaging the hull, resulting in crews beaming to safety in the emergency transporter, and scuttling the shuttle rather than trying to salvage the radioactive scrap.

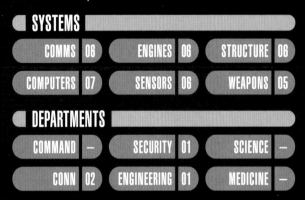

SYSTEMS

COMMS	06	ENGINES	06	STRUCTURE	06
COMPUTERS	07	SENSORS	06	WEAPONS	05

DEPARTMENTS

COMMAND	–	SECURITY	01	SCIENCE	–
CONN	02	ENGINEERING	01	MEDICINE	–

POWER: 3 **SCALE:** 1
SHIELDS: 3 **RESISTANCE:** 1

CREW COMPLEMENT: 1 or 2, plus 2 passengers

ATTACKS:
- Phaser Bank (Range Medium, 3🅰, Versatile 2)
- Escalation 2 Photon Torpedoes (Torpedo, Range Long, 4🅰 High Yield)
- Escalation 1 Single Quantum Torpedo (Torpedo, Range Long, 5🅰 High Yield, Vicious 1, Calibration)

SPECIAL RULES:
- The Type 10 is difficult to repair while in space. Any attempt to repair a Type-10 shuttle in any environment other than a shuttlebay or other repair facility increases in Difficulty by 1. Repairs made in a proper repair facility reduce in Difficulty by 1 instead.

FEDERATION ATTACK FIGHTER
ENTERED SERVICE: 2367

OVERVIEW: After the Battle of Wolf 359 and the Borg's destruction of the Sol System's fighter defense forces, designers from the Andorian Imperial Ship Yards in the Andor system proposed a desperately needed new design for a Federation strike fighter based on the popular courier

vessel also built by them. Given the unimaginative name of "Attack Fighter", many of its crews nicknamed them after the Andorian riding animal, "Zabathu."

CAPABILITIES: The fighter is small enough that it is typically piloted by a single crew member, but training flights and fighters assigned for strike missions typically have two crew assigned. Each fighter has hard-mounted two forward torpedo launchers and a single aft launcher that can double as a probe launcher or cargo delivery system. Current testing is underway on Andor to use these launchers to deliver special forces troops or undercover agents to a planet's surface where transporters aren't feasible for use and speed is more of a concern than safety. The fighter also has standard type-5 phaser strips along the edges of the vessel's warp nacelles, giving it wide firing arcs and providing accurate defensive fire against incoming heavy weapons. The fighter was never assumed to operate on its own, so the designers removed many of the original courier design's warp coils to provide extra internal space for larger fusion reactors for the impulse drive and shield emitters. This makes the fighter only able to maintain warp speeds for short durations, normally no more than thirty minutes to an hour at lower speeds, and makes it highly dependent on its parent vessel to deliver it close to the battle. As the fighter was based on an older and more reliable design, upgrading the civilian ship is fairly trivial and many Maquis cells use these upgraded vessels as attack ships in their fight against the Cardassians.

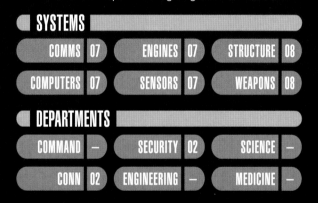

SYSTEMS

COMMS	07	ENGINES	07	STRUCTURE	08
COMPUTERS	07	SENSORS	07	WEAPONS	08

DEPARTMENTS

COMMAND	–	SECURITY	02	SCIENCE	–
CONN	02	ENGINEERING	–	MEDICINE	–

POWER: 4 **SCALE:** 2
SHIELDS: 5 **RESISTANCE:** 2

CREW COMPLEMENT: 1 or 2

ATTACKS:
- Phaser Banks (Energy, Range Close, 5🅰, Versatile 2)
- Micro-torpedoes (Torpedo, Range Long, 5🅰 High Yield)

SPECIAL RULES:
- Improved Reaction Control Systems (Talent)
- Improved Impulse Drive (Talent)

USING THE COMMAND DIVISION

3985104697936745
572821400412

USING THE COMMAND DIVISION
COMMAND DEPARTMENT STORYLINES

"YOU MADE A MILITARY DECISION TO PROTECT YOUR SHIP AND CREW. BUT YOU'RE A STARFLEET OFFICER, WORF. WE DON'T PUT CIVILIANS AT RISK — OR EVEN POTENTIALLY AT RISK — TO SAVE OURSELVES. SOMETIMES THAT MEANS WE LOSE THE BATTLE, AND SOMETIMES OUR LIVES. BUT IF YOU CAN'T MAKE THAT CHOICE, THEN YOU CAN'T WEAR THAT UNIFORM."

— CAPTAIN BENJAMIN SISKO

RED PLOT COMPONENTS

Command department officers are ideally suited for red plot components, which play to a Player Character's strengths in diplomacy, leadership, negotiation skills, and legal prowess. Effective use of red plots should help the Gamemaster provide a fun and challenging game for command Player Characters.

On one hand, playing to a command character's strengths might seem like a cop-out in that characters will do well at command-focused Tasks and challenges because that's what

they were designed to do. However, command department Players play characters that are captains and commanders because they want that sort of challenge: they want to face what Kirk, Picard, Riker, Janeway, Kira and Sisko face on a weekly basis. Why not give these Players what they want but challenge them too?

Plot components can help Gamemasters do both. A red plot component plays to a Player Character's strengths but also challenges a Player to roleplay a great moment, or come up with an innovative command-focused solution.

Use this random table to generate a quick red plot component to drop into your mission or to generate an idea to develop for your command Player Characters.

BEYOND THE FINAL FRONTIER

The *core rulebook* (page 298) suggested creating solutions to Encounters by using a color code (red solutions for command and diplomacy, gold solutions for action and combat, blue solutions for science and technological challenges). Here we present command department plot components, again coded red, gold, and blue.

- **Red plot components** focus on diplomacy, intrigue, first contact, political storylines, legal stories, and anything of a spiritual nature that doesn't fit in science.

- **Gold plot components** involve combat (personal or ship), physical action and activities, some intrigue or espionage, and some action-oriented technological storylines.

- **Blue plot components** focus on science or medical issues, engineering and technological issues, and tactical scenarios that don't fit easily into a gold component.

GENERATING RED PLOT COMPONENTS

D20 ROLL	RED PLOT COMPONENT
1	Conspiracy
2–6	Diplomacy
7–11	First Contact
12–14	Political
15–17	Show the Flag
18–19	Spiritual
20	Starfleet JAG

CONSPIRACY

While the Federation and Starfleet strive to build and protect a utopian society, there have been conspiracies buried deep in both over the life of the *Star Trek* franchise. A group of Starfleet admirals secretly allied with Klingon and Romulan adversaries to keep the war between their peoples going, and to assassinate key personalities on both sides (*Star Trek VI*). An alien parasite infected someone deep within Starfleet Command and nearly succeeded in destabilizing and taking over the Federation (*The Next Generation* episode "Conspiracy"). A Dominion Founder Changeling infiltrated Starfleet Command and attempted to destabilize the Federation (*Deep Space Nine* two-part arc "Homefront" and "Paradise Lost").

These examples show that conspiracies in a ***Star Trek Adventures*** campaign are viable plot options. One way to use a conspiracy storyline would be as a string of components related to a conspiracy, with each adding another piece to the puzzle. The first component could be dropped into a mission as a single-scene moment for a Player Character (e.g. the Chief Engineer gets a cryptic message from an old Academy friend but is unable to follow up on the message). In a later mission, the old friend meets the Chief Engineer and works with them in a B-plot. Subsequently the Academy friend goes missing and solving that mystery becomes the main storyline.

DIPLOMACY

Many *Star Trek* episodes involve diplomacy at one level or another, and many imply that diplomatic events occur off-camera or after the crisis has been resolved. Players may not want to do trade negotiations, but the dramatic events leading up to talks could be a plot component.

For example, in an episode with a new race you could the put the captain and crew at odds with the alien crew, and then resolve the episode on a positive note. In a later B-plot component or a character-specific scene, follow up the connection. Perhaps the alien captain calls in a favor or makes a request, and the Starfleet captain decides to personally help the alien captain.

This leads to another A-plot episode where the captain plays a key role at the talks that bring her friend and ally into a formal trade relationship with the Federation (or fails to do so), based on the actions of the players. Expanding plot components helps Players feel that what they do during a given session, and the actions their characters take, matter in the setting you are building. It will remind Players that actions have consequences, even if they assume they'll never see a particular planet, ally or adversary again.

FIRST CONTACT

Much like the above, first contact is a good plot component if you set up the situation in an earlier episode, and then build on it in later plot components. These can be another A-story, a B-plot involving the newly-contacted species, or a character-specific moment where a Player Character takes some personal time to go touch base with the contacted

race as they learn about the Federation. It could be that the Player Character is the only Federation member trusted by the new aliens, and they specifically request that Character be present.

First contact missions and plot components are particularly well-suited for captain and commander characters, since negotiation and interpersonal relationships are generally a key part of the characters' ethos. First contact missions are also well-suited for introducing or using the social conflict skills, presented in the *core rulebook* (page 164) and in this book's Chapter 5.3.

POLITICAL

The *Next Generation*, and *Deep Space Nine* in particular, were strong in politically-focused episodes and plotlines. *Deep Space Nine* was deeply involved with Bajoran politics and religion and their interaction with Cardassian political and military events. Captain Picard, through a series of plot moments, became the arbiter of succession for the Klingon Empire: a highly unusual situation where a Starfleet officer affected the leadership of an alien species.

Using political plot components, Federation or alien, is a great way to get Player Characters involved in worlds that are not necessarily their own. For example, a sciences

officer becomes best friends with another species' sciences officer during a disastrous meeting turned positive; that officer becomes the primary point of contact for the Federation with that alien species. If that species then goes on to broker deals with the Federation, the sciences officer might be called to the negotiations due to their personal connections. The task may be well outside the scope of their skillset, but it provides an interesting challenge for Player and character.

SHOW THE FLAG

Sometimes the Federation needs to remind a colony or outlying member world about why they are members of the Federation. This is not military posturing, but a diplomatic visit that reminds the world of the benefits of the Federation. Sometimes, it's necessary to lay claim to a planet, moon, or spatial feature; this may involve reminding an alien species or marauder group that a somewhere is, in fact, claimed by the Federation.

A show the flag plot component could turn into something even more meaningful if the captain and the NPC antagonists continue to interact over the course of several missions. You could use the storyline as B- or C-plot components for several missions, and then turn the connection between the captain and the world into a fully realized primary plot for a later mission, building on the smaller components in the plot arc.

SPIRITUAL

Spiritual plot components, such as visions that Captain Sisko or Chakotay experience during their respective series, can be command-style plot components because: they don't really fit anywhere else; and command department officers are strong in command-focused Attributes and Disciplines. Captain Sisko's visions as the Emissary of the Prophets tied directly into his role as commander of *DS9*. His visions affected his command decisions and the recommendations he made to Starfleet and the Federation. Without those spiritual moments, his decisions could have had a more significant impact on both Bajor and the Federation. It is these types of experiences and potential consequences that many Players love in a mission and campaign.

There is no formalized religion within the Federation, and individual citizens are free to make their own choices about faith and religion. Many alien species bring their own world's religious practices with them as they serve in Starfleet. Although the Federation might not have an official faith or denomination, alien worlds do and Player Characters from one of those alien species will want to practice their faith.

As long as they are respectfully handled, plot components revolving around faith issues and questions can generate powerful stories. There are plenty of real-world religious texts and stories to draw upon for plot component ideas.

EPISODES FOCUSED ON COMMAND CHALLENGES

"COGENITOR" (ENTERPRISE)
Captain Archer and the crew of the *Enterprise* must navigate a delicate first contact situation when Commander Tucker interferes with the natural order of the Vissians.

"BALANCE OF TERROR" (THE ORIGINAL SERIES)
Captain Kirk engages in a battle of wills and well-matched starships against a worthy Romulan adversary.

"THE BEST OF BOTH WORLDS, PART I" (THE NEXT GENERATION)
Captain Picard and then Commander Riker make hard command choices while the *Enterprise*-D engages the implacable Borg.

"IN THE PALE MOONLIGHT" (DEEP SPACE NINE)
Captain Sisko navigates a slippery moral slope to determine if the ends justify the means of pulling the Romulans into the conflict with the Dominion.

"CARETAKER" (VOYAGER)
Captain Janeway must pull a disparate group together into a functional crew when the *U.S.S. Voyager* is stranded some 70,000 light years away from home.

CONSEQUENCES OF BREACHING THE PRIME DIRECTIVE

If a Player Character breaches the Prime Directive during a mission, you as the Gamemaster should be prepared to add a scene involving an investigation into the breach, or plan a scene for the next mission that focuses on investigating the Player Character and their actions that led to the breach. A captain of a starship is responsible for the actions of its crew, so any officer's poor handling of the Prime Directive will directly involve the captain as well.

In game terms, a breach of the Prime Directive negatively impacts a Player Character's Reputation Check (*Star Trek Adventures* core rulebook p. 295). In addition, that Player Character's captain or commanding officer also has their Reputation Check negatively impacted. Additional consequences may arise from the breach, including the disciplinary measures detailed in the core rulebook. You should be careful when handing out disciplinary measures, as one Player Character impacting another Player Character may create hard feelings among the players, and demoting a Player Character or removing a Player Character from command may create an untenable situation for the continuation of your campaign.

STARFLEET JAG

As with diplomacy components, any story line involving the Judge Advocate General's Office (JAG), is ripe with possibilities. Captain Picard had a connection to the JAG officer that came to Lieutenant Commander Data's hearing in "Measure of a Man," and that sort of personal dynamic can play itself out over several plot components.

The JAG is often involved in disciplinary hearings against Starfleet officers, and where Federation citizens or non-Federation citizens level charges against Starfleet officers. These actions can take the form of an adventure plotline or could be used as plot components. For example, the crew solves a problem on an alien planet in one mission. In a later mission, a wronged representative of the alien species contacts the local Starfleet JAG office and demands that the captain be apprehended for improper behavior. The next mission now has a B-plot involving the captain's hearing before a JAG officer.

Some involved situations or hearings could result in a court-martial proceeding for a Player Character. If this occurs in your game, review the discussion of courts-martial on page 296 of the *core rulebook*.

BLUE PLOT COMPONENTS

These are plot components for command department characters focused on sciences and technology. As with the red components they can be used "as is" or adjusted to fit a different character. While command characters are not ideally suited for blue components, every Starfleet officer is cross-trained and this ensures that every Player Character, no matter their focus, could attempt a plot component not keyed to their particular department or division. Giving a command character a blue plot component presents a fun challenge to the Player and Player Character.

Use this random table to generate a quick blue plot component to drop into your mission, or to generate an idea for a new blue plot component to develop for your command Player Characters.

GENERATING BLUE PLOT COMPONENTS

D20 ROLL	BLUE PLOT COMPONENT
1–5	Deep Space Exploration
6–7	Evacuation
8–9	Medical Issue
10–14	Near Space Exploration
15–17	Planetary Exploration
18–20	Research

DEEP SPACE EXPLORATION

Deep space exploration is largely why Starfleet exists. Venturing into the great unknown, discovering new worlds and interacting with unknown alien species is the bread and butter of Starfleet's mandate from the Federation.

This type of plot or subplot is ideal for captains and commanders because it gives them an opportunity to feel the weight of command. In deep space, far from a starbase or the watchful eye of Starfleet, the captain is the voice of the Federation. On the edge of space, any number of aliens might encounter the ship and crew, and the captain will be viewed as the authority figure and representative of the entire Federation.

EVACUATION

An episode involving the evacuation of a planet, starbase, or ship could impact a command level officer depending on how events progress. He could be lauded as a hero, or damned as a failure for not getting enough people evacuated. Survivors can recur in B-plots or character stories, either delivering praise or attempting revenge.

There's also the opportunity for a command character to plan how to make an evacuation happen. Some Players love to work out the logistics of such a task, and you could play that up by using some of the mechanics presented in the core rulebook to help develop the plot component around the evacuation, and add in some subplot possibilities connected to the evacuation.

MEDICAL

A medical crisis on a planet or starbase could cause a captain or commander to be put in a situation where she has to use her leadership abilities to keep a society together in the face of disaster, such as the outbreak of a plague or a strange biological agent ripping through a community. A command character could be tested through their negotiation skills, as well as their ability to keep a frightened mob from rioting or jumping to a wrong conclusion.

NEAR SPACE EXPLORATION

This plot component category includes those story ideas and plot hooks that revolve around known areas of the Alpha and Beta Quadrants. Much of *The Next Generation* regularly revisited known areas of the two quadrants, such as Earth, Romulus, and Qo'noS, particularly with Worf's character arc involving the Klingon High Council, the

House of Duras, and Chancellor Gowron. Your command character can get involved with one or more of the known Federation worlds, and develop a personal or professional relationship with an alien species. If a scientific or medical discovery or issue arose, the ship and crew could be dispatched to deal with it, leveraging the personal connection to the aliens.

PLANETARY EXPLORATION

Planetary exploration is just as important as deep space exploration. Ancient civilizations, artifacts, scientific discoveries buried under (kilo)meters of rock, and scientific discoveries can be found on planets just as easily as in space. This plot component category could also encompass exploration of moons, asteroid belts, plasma fields, and other solid stellar phenomena.

Example: *A captain or commander placed in charge of a planetary exploration mission might find the ruins of an ancient civilization, the living descendants of an alien race long marooned on the planet, or valuable mineral deposits that might be claimed by the Federation or nearby Federation ally or member world. The commanding officer's reports and recommendations regarding the planet would carry significant weight with the Federation Council.*

RESEARCH

A catch-all category that encompasses all research and development that might involve a command-level officer, either because they are personally interested in the research (such as Captain Picard taking on Professor Galen's search in "The Chase") or because they want to champion someone else's research and development efforts.

Example: *The sciences chief aboard the U.S.S. Garrett begins a long-term research project involving tetryon particles and their possible connection to a warp-field upgrade. The Garrett's executive officer, a former engineer, supports the sciences chief's experiments and related requests for sensor pallet time when possible. She puts in good word with her contacts at the Cochrane Institute, enabling the sciences chief to deepen his research.*

GOLD PLOT COMPONENTS

Below are plot components for command department characters focused on, or that could result in, physical action, and starship-oriented combat. As with the red and blue plot components, they can be used "as is" or adjusted to fit a particular character. Command characters are normally tactically cross-trained since they will often be leaders during an engagement. This means that, while command characters may not always be the focus of a gold plot component, they may well possess the skills needed to tackle a gold component. A command character might possess special knowledge of an alien species, adversary, or region of space that might help them effectively deal with a gold plot.

Use the table to generate a quick gold plot component for your mission, or to generate an idea for a new plot to develop for your command Player Characters.

GENERATING GOLD PLOT COMPONENTS

D20 ROLL	GOLD PLOT COMPONENT
1–5	Defense
6–9	Escort
10–12	Espionage
13–16	Patrol
17–20	Tactical

DEFENSE

Any number of plot hooks and episodes can involve the concept of defense, whether it's protecting the Federation or a member world; personal defense protecting an individual or group; or defending a ship from some strange sentient entity. Defense plot components also include missions that involve defending someone, something, or even a principle or Value, such as the Federation, the Prime Directive, an alien race's rights or laws, or some other law or tenet important to the command Player Character.

Example: *Following negotiations held onboard her ship, a Starfleet captain is asked to provide security for the alien diplomats. Because of the captain's personal connection to the alien species and their homeworld, she is singled out as trustworthy. Determined to maintain and enhance the relationship between the aliens and the Federation, the captain assigns herself and her Security Chief to the task, despite her First Officer's concerns.*

ESCORT

Space is so vast that it is easy for smugglers, pirates, and adversaries to hide effectively, and conduct hit-and-run attacks on the Federation and shipping lanes. Starfleet vessels are often assigned to escort duties: shepherding transports, providing additional security for diplomatic delegates, or escorting something or somebody of value from one planet to another.

Example: *The U.S.S. Thunderchild, and its Klingon counterpart, the I.K.S. Mupwl', are assigned to escort a convoy from Narendra Station through the largely uncharted Shackleton Expanse to a deep space listening post.*

ESPIONAGE

With the existence of secret and not-so-secret organizations such as the Tal Shiar, the Obsidian Order, the Orion Syndicate and countless others, it's often necessary for Starfleet personnel to conduct secret operations and missions, sometimes off the record and without formal recognizance. While many on the Federation and Security Councils frown on such under-the-table actions, others in the high command are well aware that spying is part of doing business on the galactic scale.

Example: *In* The Next Generation *episode "Chain of Command," Captain Picard, Lt. Commander Worf, and Doctor Crusher train on the holodeck to infiltrate a Cardassian facility. (Picard was chosen because of his experience with theta-band carrier waves).*

PATROL

Patrol missions involve surveying an area, reporting and investigating any strange events, anomalies, or suspicious behavior. In addition to the Romulan Neutral Zone and the Cardassian Demilitarized Zone, the Federation shares border hotspots with other spacefaring races, and each border needs to be monitored just in case something untoward occurs.

Example: *The U.S.S. Athena is assigned to the Badlands, along the Demilitarized Zone between Cardassian and Federation space, to monitor possible Cardassian military actions and any possible Maquis terrorist efforts. The Athena is given this assignment because her captain is* *familiar with Cardassian tactics and military tendencies, and Starfleet feels his expertise will prove valuable along the border.*

experienced officer's tactical insights into an alien species or a specific part of space can often be the difference between victory and defeat.

TACTICAL

During periods of tension or outright warfare, Starfleet posts experienced, knowledgeable officers to the front lines, to use the best possible personnel in the right circumstances to achieve the Federation's goals, or a victory. An

Example: *Commander Kevin Traynor, executive officer of the U.S.S. Athena, is temporarily re-assigned to Admiral Ross's wartime staff. His advanced tactical acumen and experience fighting the Cardassians over the course of many conflicts bring many benefits.*

USING THE COMMAND DIVISION
CONN DEPARTMENT STORYLINES

RED PLOT COMPONENTS

Conn department officers are well-suited for red plot components, as they play to a conn-level Player Character's cross-training in leadership and diplomacy, and their foundation Starfleet training. Effective use of red plot components should help a Gamemaster provide a fun and challenging game for conn Player Characters beyond just navigating a starship or piloting support craft.

Use the table to generate a red plot component to drop into a mission or to generate an idea to develop for conn Player Characters.

GENERATING RED PLOT COMPONENTS

D20 ROLL	RED PLOT COMPONENT
1	Conspiracy
2–6	Diplomacy
7–11	First Contact
12–14	Political
15–17	Show the Flag
18–19	Spiritual
20	Starfleet JAG

BEYOND THE FINAL FRONTIER

This subchapter builds on the plot component concept presented in Chapter 5.1 and provides brief descriptions of plot components specifically focused on conn department officers.

CONSPIRACY

While the Federation and Starfleet strive to build and protect a utopian society, there have been conspiracies deep within the system during the life of the *Star Trek* franchise. Several examples were presented in Chapter 5.1. A conn officer might learn of a conspiracy while serving at the conn station on the bridge during a tense conversation between the captain and an incoming caller, or could be serving as a personal shuttle pilot for a high-level functionary at the heart of a conspiracy.

DIPLOMACY

Many *Star Trek* episodes involve diplomacy at one level or another, and many imply the existence of diplomatic events off-camera. A conn officer might be on the bridge when her commanding officer negotiates across subspace, may ferry dignitaries from the ship to talks, or might have a personal stake in diplomatic negotiations thanks to their background or history.

FIRST CONTACT

Thanks to their cross-training, conn officers often make good landing party or away team members. A conn officer with a particular background or skill set might prove valuable during a first contact mission.

POLITICAL

As with many of other plot ideas, a conn officer's background, and set of Values and Talents, may mean the conn officer is conversant with local or Federation politics involving a particular alien species. In such cases, a conn officer might offer more than only acting as navigator or helmsman.

SHOW THE FLAG

Sometimes the Federation needs to go to a colony or member world and remind people why they are belong to the Federation. Depending on whether the mission involves the conn officer's starship or a shuttle, she could be right in the middle of the action, whether on the bridge or actively piloting the shuttle to a destination.

SPIRITUAL

A conn officer's background, Values and Talents may result in the conn officer having a particular spiritual outlook, religion, or set of beliefs that shape who they are just as much as their Starfleet oath and Federation service. If their faith has any outward trappings, such as a head cloth or an earring (the Bajorans, for example), the conn officer's placement on the bridge might ease communications between the bridge crew and an alien species being contacted.

STARFLEET JAG

Story lines involving Starfleet's Judge Advocate General's Office (JAG), are full of possibilities. The JAG is often involved in disciplinary hearings against Starfleet officers, and when Federation citizens or outsiders bring charges against Starfleet officers. These events can be a mission plotline, or used as plot components. A conn officer might serve as a witness, or may be the subject of the hearing: conn officers are usually in the thick of things because of their duties on the bridge and diverse skills.

BLUE PLOT COMPONENTS

These plot components for conn department characters focus on sciences and technology. As with red and gold plot components, they can be used "as is" or adjusted to fit a character. Conn officers are usually cross-trained, and they may be well-suited to tackle any plot component. Assigning a conn character a blue plot component could be a welcome change of pace for the Player Character.

Use the table to generate a quick blue plot component to drop into a mission or to kickstart an idea to develop for conn Player Characters.

EPISODES FOCUSED ON CONN CHALLENGES

"MINEFIELD" (ENTERPRISE)

When the *Enterprise* is trapped in a Romulan minefield and Lieutenant Reed is trapped on the hull of the starship, Ensign Mayweather must carefully navigate the ship out of the minefield to protect both his crewmate and the ship.

"THE CORBOMITE MANEUVER" (THE ORIGINAL SERIES)

When the *Enterprise* encounters a strange object in space, Lieutenant Sulu displays versatility in covering for his fellow navigator Bailey and then moves the starship through some fancy maneuvers against the *Fesarius*.

"BOOBY TRAP" (THE NEXT GENERATION)

Captain Picard uses some clever helmsman tricks to try and pull the *Enterprise*-D out of an ancient trap.

"THE SIEGE" (DEEP SPACE NINE)

Major Kira and Lieutenant Dax work together to jury-rig an aged Bajoran sub-impulse raider and fly it through myriad challenges.

"EXTREME RISK" (VOYAGER)

Lieutenant Paris and the crew of *Voyager* race to complete the *Delta Flyer* before the Malons can complete construction of their shuttle.

GENERATING BLUE PLOT COMPONENTS

D20 ROLL	BLUE PLOT COMPONENT
1–5	Deep Space Exploration
6–7	Evacuation
8–9	Medical Issue
10–14	Near Space Exploration
15–17	Planetary Exploration
18–20	Research

DEEP SPACE EXPLORATION

Starfleet exists to do deep space exploration: the great unknown, discovering new worlds and interacting with alien species are the basis of all Federation's instructions to Starfleet.

This plot type is ideal for conn officers because it gives them the opportunity to pilot their vessels into uncharted territory, often unaccompanied by any other Federation starship. Many pilots like to have bragging rights that they were first (within Starfleet at least) to navigate a previously-unexplored spatial phenomena.

EVACUATION

An episode involving the evacuation of a planet, starbase, or ship could impact a conn officer because, depending on how the evacuation goes, he could be the hero of the hour or a failure who killed too many people. Survivors, brimming with gratitude or hungry for revenge, can recur in B-plots or character stories.

There's also the chance for a conn character to plan the evacuation. The logistics of the operation will appeal to some, you can use the mechanics presented in the core rulebook to develop the evacuation and subplot possibilities. A conn officer might produce an innovative evacuation plan involving shuttles and transporter relays, for example.

MEDICAL ISSUE

A planetary or starbase medical crisis could mean a conn officer is put in a situation where she has to use her cross-training to hold a society together. The outbreak of a plague or a sudden, strange biological event will test the bonds of any group. The conn character, removed from the pilot's seat, can be tested in ways that create growth opportunities for the character.

Example: *A conn officer is on a planet when a plague breaks out. She refuses to shuttle any of her crewmates back to the ship for fear of spreading the plague. The conn officer attempts to use of her medical training and nascent engineering talents by constructing triage centres in nearby villages until a cure is found.*

NEAR SPACE EXPLORATION

This category includes those story ideas and plot hooks involving the Alpha and Beta Quadrants; *The Next*

Generation regularly revisited these quadrants, and places such as Earth, Romulus, and Qo'noS. A conn character can get involved with Federation worlds; develop personal or professional relationships with an alien species; and become familiar with a particular system or spatial phenomena such as the Briar Patch or the Badlands. If a scientific or medical issue arises, the conn officer's personal links make it sensible to send her ship and crew to deal with events.

PLANETARY EXPLORATION

Planetary exploration is an important aspect of deep space exploration, because it's on planets that the ruins of ancient civilizations, artifacts, scientific and other mysteries buried by the ages can be found. This plot component also includes exploration of moons, asteroids, and any other solid stellar system phenomena. A conn officer could well be responsible for transporting away teams, carrying supplies, and reconnaissance missions, using shuttles and other small support craft.

RESEARCH

This covers any research and development where a senior officer might be involved, either through personal interest or because they are encouraging another's efforts.

One way to involve a conn officer in a science officer's research project is for the conn officer to plot the orbital position that gives the best sensor readings for a given experiment. Even when a ship assumes a standard orbit, the conn officer can orient the ship in such a way that sensor pallets can be brought into play, allowing science teams to conduct experiments even as the main plot of the mission is underway.

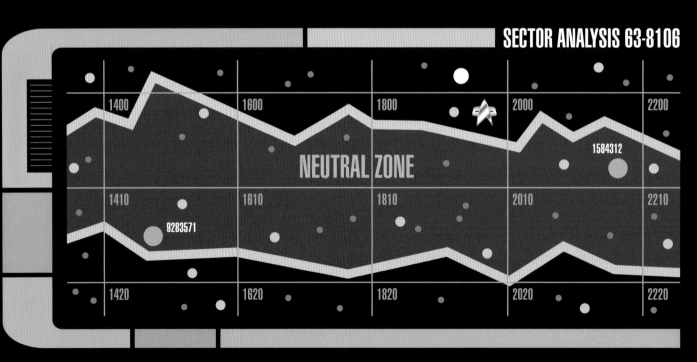

SECTOR ANALYSIS 63-8106

NEUTRAL ZONE

GOLD PLOT COMPONENTS

These gold plot components for conn department characters concentrate on combat and , physical action at the personal and ship levels. As with other components, they can be used as they stand or adjusted to fit a different character. Conn characters are cross-trained in tactical procedures since they are usually at the controls when their starship is in combat. They have a good understanding of best practice where Starfleet tactics are concerned, and understand the tactical nuances of adversary species. Conn officers often attend advanced tactical training courses, and some transfer to the tactical department during their careers from junior officers to capable leaders and eventually commanders and captains. It is not unknown for conn characters to possess special knowledge of alien species, adversaries, or space region that give them an edge when dealing with a gold plot component.

The table will help generate a gold plot component for a mission, or generate an idea for whole new plot development for conn Player Characters.

GENERATING GOLD PLOT COMPONENTS

D20 ROLL	GOLD PLOT COMPONENT
1–5	Defense
6–9	Escort
10–12	Espionage
13–16	Patrol
17–20	Tactical

DEFENSE

A large number of plots and episodes can involve defensive actions of some kind. These can be as large as protecting the Federation, or as small and intimate as guarding one person, a group or a single ship. The defensive element can also be abstract: the defense of an ideal, a principle or a value, such as the Prime Directive or an alien species' rites and rituals. Defense of an abstact is usually better when the concept is important to the Player Character.

Conn officers are trained in tactical combat maneuvers, and a defense plot component may well require those skills be used to the full. The speed at which a conn officer can carry out a maneuver, and if she can effectively anticipate a captain's orders may mean the difference between a success and a wrecked starship.

ESCORT

Starfleet vessels are often assigned to escort duties. Space has plenty of empty places for smugglers, pirates, and enemies (open and covert) to hide and launch raids. Shepherding transports from one planet to another may not seem glamorous or exciting, but it is vital work. And it is work that can quickly lose any hint of boredom.

Conn officers may pilot a starship as part of escort duties, but they might also suggest escort patterns, convoy speeds and courses, and other tactical ideas to help move the transports and escorts to their destination. Many conn officers excel in finding shortcuts through stellar cartography, and such knowledge has helped dozens of transports and convoys avoid naural phenomena and raider ambushes.

ESPIONAGE

Ever-present threats such as the Tal Shiar, the Obsidian Order, the Orion Syndicate and other secret organizations make it necessary for Starfleet personnel to carry out secret missions. These are often off the record and without formal approval. The Federation Council and the Security Council may not like such shadowy actions, but others within the Federation structure consider them utterly necessary.

Conn officers can be ideal agents. Sometimes the humble pilot of a shuttle or hopper goes unnoticed, and that anonymity is a spy's stock-in-trade. Anyone transporting military officials or political leaders could well overhear critical information. Plenty of commanding officers take open hails on the bridge, and sensitive information can be overheard by the entire bridge crew. If the conn officer on the bridge happens to be a spy, they can gather significant intelligence without too much risk.

CAPTAIN'S LOG

CAPTAIN'S LOG, STARDATE 1416.4

Ensign Kuvash was visibly shaken as she walked into my office, a rare sight for the Efrosion. I couldn't cut her some slack, unfortunately, and from the very beginning I had to highlight the importance of the miscalculation she made in plotting a course in low orbit.

By descending into the mesosphere, we risked detection not only from any rudimentary radar systems but to visual detection too. Any member of the native species with anything greater than a simple binocular lens could have seen us. While the mission to salvage the malfunctioning probe – and therefore solving the crisis she helped create – was imperative, it was too daring a maneuver for such a task.

I've asked Lt. Commander Daldry to monitor and translate any signals coming from the surface. With an established press in the native society, it wouldn't surprise me if UFO stories, like those of 20th century Earth, were to surface shortly.

— Captain Rinix, *U.S.S. Oldfield*

PATROL

Patrols involve reporting and investigating any strange events, anomalies, or suspicious behavior within an assigned area. The Romulan Neutral Zone and the Cardassian Demilitarized Zone are always heavily patrolled, but the Federation has other hot-spots on other borders, and all need watching to a lesser extent. After all, small problems that are properly monitored can be dealt with before they become serious problems.

A conn officer might have an influence on where their ship is posted: familiarity with an area is always an advantage.

Example: *A conn officer who spent time on the Cardassian border throwing a shuttle around plasma eddies might be the perfect guide in the Badlands. Starfleet would use the officer's local knowledge to help detect and catch Maquis fighters.*

TACTICAL

During times of war, or even limited hostilities, Starfleet tries to make sure experienced officers are on the front lines. Every advantage might be the one that brings victory, or at least avoids defeat. An officer's insights into the local 'geography of space' might suggest all kinds of tactical ruses.

Example: *A conn officer's has extensive experience and a hobby of piloting Klingon birds-of-prey in simulations. Starfleet takes note of these skills, and recommends the officers for secondment to the Klingon Defense Force. The officer takes advantage of the transfer to learn all he can about Klingon navigation techniques and combat maneuvering.*

USING THE COMMAND DIVISION
SOCIAL CONFLICTS

DIPLOMATIC PROTOCOL

Peaceful coexistence between worlds, species, and cultures is a primary goal for the United Federation of Planets. It is so central that all Starfleet officers are given diplomatic protocol training, and many officers develop these skills during their careers. Command officers, given that they are representatives of their ships, Starfleet, and the Federation, are expected to be diplomatic, even if they are not diplomats.

All through Starfleet history different captains have remarked on this fact. All consider this a natural responsibility: some hold that they are not diplomats; others hold that the diplomatic work of Starfleet is a

sacred duty. Whatever the case, many diplomatic missions are facilitated by Starfleet even as the Federation provides an abundance of ambassadors, envoys, and negotiators.

This chapter refines the Social Conflict rules (page 164 in the *Star Trek Adventures* core rulebook), and provides additional guidelines and suggestions for how to use them for protracted, intense, high-stakes diplomatic action, negotiations, and similar situations. This chapter is mainly for the use of the Gamemaster, but there's nothing in here that Players mustn't see.

USING TRAITS

As covered in the core rulebook, the Gamemaster can make use of Traits to shape and define scenes, situations, and environments. While long-term persistent Traits on

characters are typically reserved for major, definitive, and often permanent aspects of a character's nature, that doesn't mean that characters cannot have short-term Traits applied during a scene.

This is a useful way for the Gamemaster to call attention to specific beliefs, perceptions, strong emotions, and other factors that may affect a character's behavior, particularly how they'll respond to persuasion and coercion. Using Traits in this way relies on the fact that a Trait only remains in place as long as it is true; short-term personal Traits can highlight things that may only be true for a character for a single scene (or less). A Klingon may gain *Enraged* as a Trait during a social conflict but when the Klingon calms down it disappears. There may be potential to calm the Klingon down during the scene to salvage the attempted interaction.

This can be a valuable tool for running a Social Conflict: a few Traits to emphasize moods, feelings, expectations, and "in the moment" details can be guidance for setting the Difficulty of Persuade Tasks and the use of Social Tools. They may even determine if some options are possible at a specific moment, and provide a rough map for how things could play out. Traits can be added and removed because of actions taken within the Social Conflict: a failed attempt to deceive may anger the target, making them less willing to cooperate in future; a target who becomes curious may be amenable to extra persuasion.

In these situations, a character's Values can also be used as if they were Traits. Values represent the character's fundamental beliefs and significant drives, and should have an impact upon social interactions. A character with a deep loathing for Romulans is unlikely to be able to treat with them peacefully, and certainly won't be receptive to their requests.

Of course, while some emotions, beliefs, and so forth may be obvious to anyone nearby, others may be harder to discern. The Gamemaster does not have to have every personal Trait known to the players, particularly if they represent a belief or perception, or their target is especially good at hiding or controlling their emotional state. This can add to a Social Conflict if characters need to spend effort trying to figure out their target's feelings and perspectives. Attempting to discern someone's feelings may involve a Task to read their body language or responses; engaging with them to subtly get them to reveal something; or research based on previous encounters. Any of these might require a Task (**Insight + Command** is a good combination to use) or even an Opposed Task if the target is deliberately reserved.

STRUCTURING A SOCIAL CONFLICT

The Social Conflict section in the core rulebook (page 164) provides information about the tools that characters use during social conflict. It's the Gamemaster who creates the problems those tools are designed to solve. This requires a degree of planning from the Gamemaster and some improvisational skills.

At their simplest, Social Conflicts are one party's goal or request which another party can prevent or permit. The conflict is resolved through the Persuade Task: can one party convince the other to grant a request, or not? Everything else — deception, intimidation, negotiation, and evidence — exists to support that idea, shaping the Persuade Task's context. A Klingon captain may not pay the proper respect convinced some is worthy, while a Ferengi trader is easier to deal with when there's profit involved.

A single Persuade Task isn't sufficient to handle involved situations. It is at this point that some additional structure is needed.

CHALLENGES IN SOCIAL CONFLICT
The simplest way to expand social conflicts is to use Challenges (page 89 of the core rulebook), with the situation requiring multiple Persuade Tasks and each Persuade Task serving as a single Key Task for the Challenge. Use of the social tools is, as always, supplementary: they exist to influence the difficulty and possibility of Persuade Tasks.

Unlike a normal Challenge, one used in a Social Conflict context may not necessarily relate each Key Task to a specific activity. Instead, it's often better if each represents a

The Galaxy is not short of individuals with mental powers, and many have served in Starfleet over the centuries. It's worth spending time to consider how such powers affect social conflict and other situations, as they can often overwhelm an unprepared Gamemaster.

Part of the key to understanding telepathy's possibilities and limitations is that, in the Federation, telepathy is not mysterious or mystical. It is a scientific fact and a natural part of the neurobiology of several species (Betazoids and Vulcans, and even Trill symbionts). There are extensive scientific and medical texts about telepaths and their abilities. It is a known quantity. Telepathy is not even limited to those species. It crops up in many species, though telepaths in non-telepathic species have difficulties during development unless they seek out specialized training. Amongst telepathic species, there are laws, traditions, and taboos that govern telepathy and, as with any ability, skill and experience are important in using it effectively.

Telepathic minds perceive some of the "psionic field", much as eyes perceive a portion of the electromagnetic spectrum, and ears can discern sonic vibrations. This field is influenced by the mental activity of most living beings and a telepath learns how to interpret the unique fluctuations and variations in the psionic field caused by the thoughts and emotions of others. Some species, such as Ferengi, Dopterians, and Changelings, have a different neurobiology that prevents their minds being read by telepath.

Practically, telepathy comes into two broad categories: communication and perception.

Communication normally comes in a form like speech: speaking with the mind rather than the voice. This takes little effort by the telepath, but conveying complex or detailed information, such as imagery, sensory information, or even memories, requires significantly more effort (such as a Task). Communication is easier with other telepaths and empaths, and with family members, close friends, and lovers. Two-way communication with non-telepaths takes more concentration, as the telepath sends a message, then reads the recipient's mind for a response.

Perception is the telepathic sensing of surface thoughts and emotions. However, just as concentration is needed to hear a specific conversation in a crowded room, it takes skill and clarity of mind to pick up specific thoughts from the 'background noise' of nearby minds. Unskilled or especially-powerful telepaths can find themselves overwhelmed by the minds around them, especially during tense or high-pressure situations. Sensing beyond surface thoughts to read something deeper takes effort and concentration.

This is easier if the subject is familiar or telepathic. Technology exists that can interfere with telepathy, though outright blocking is difficult. Strong willed or disciplined individuals can prevent their minds being read entirely. Delving too deeply and without consent into another mind is regarded as a serious crime by many telepathic species, and telepathic evidence is not considered definitive in Federation law courts.

Telepathy can place suggestions, mental illusions, and altered memories into a mind and so influence a subject. These actions are difficult and dangerous, and normally only performed by extremely powerful telepaths. These are regarded as a violent intrusion and an assault unless performed with consent. Because of the nature of these activities, consent is harder to determine (as mind and memory may be altered) and their use is hard to justify morally or ethically.

Some technologies can mimic telepathic perception in a limited way, though these tend to be invasive and painful, and only used for interrogations. They're used extensively by the Romulans and the Breen, though the Klingons have been known to use such techniques as well.

EMPATHY

Though like telepathy, empathy is limited to discerning emotions. This can make it easier to use, but there is only so much information that can be gleaned from knowing someone's emotional state. It therefore requires skill to use effectively. Empaths have a small degree of telepathic ability, sufficient to use simple communication with telepaths, close friends, and family.

TACTILE TELEPATHY

As practiced by Vulcans, tactile telepathy — the mind-meld — requires physical contact; with greater effort and difficulty close physical proximity may also work. Mind-melds are extremely powerful, allowing Vulcans to share thoughts, memories, and experiences with another with far greater speed and efficiency than, say Betazoid telepathy. However, this closeness makes it physically and mentally dangerous, and it often has lasting repercussions even if performed properly. Because of this, and the risks of an improperly-performed meld, Vulcans do not carry out mind-melds without proper training (the *Mind-Meld* talent). Even then, they will do it with good reason, especially with a member of another species. Contact with an emotionally-volatile mind can be particularly dangerous.

The Elder Assembly today released the news that the object seen in the sky on the early morning of the Day of the Julani was in fact one of their own new sky craft! I call that ridiculous! Unidentified Sky Entity is what I declare it! Completely unknown! And not from our world!

I believe, like many who live on the southern shores of our beautiful state, that this thing is an entity of alien origin! Don't trust me, fellow Slauarilians? Look to the skies tonight and seek out the same entity – a disk with two tail-like cylinders behind! They will be back, I promise you that.

single obstacle or barrier between the Player Characters and their ultimate goal. These obstacles may be steps to be taken before the next obstacle is confronted. A good example might be matters of trust and respect: each successive Key Task that a Player Character completes means the target trusts or respects the Character a little more, opening options and approaches at each step. Alternatively, they may be a need for the Player Character to convince a target of the Character's value or usefulness. Each obstacle is largely independent from the others, requiring their own approaches, activities, and use of social tools and other methods to influence each Persuade Task.

As with Challenges, this could be used to structure an individual scene, or it could be used to provide a structure for several scenes over a protracted period, depending on what the Social Conflict represents. An intense negotiation may have several distinct obstacles to overcome all within a single scene, while infiltration into an enemy group might spread obstacles over several scenes.

Example: *Chief O'Brien is undercover for Starfleet Intelligence to infiltrate part of the Orion Syndicate. This will be a long and difficult process. The Syndicate are suspicious of everyone, and have no reason to trust O'Brien. The Gamemaster establishes three obstacles for O'Brien: "become known to the Syndicate", "be invited to join the Syndicate", and "gain the trust of someone in the Syndicate", after which O'Brien should be well-placed to get any information he wants.*

O'Brien has identified a group of Syndicate operatives in a bar — Flith, Krole, and their leader, Liam Bilby — and Krole goes to use a comm booth to charge their meals to someone else. Although the syndicate members don't know it, O'Brien booby-trapped the comm booth; when Krole connects his dataport, he's struck by a powerful electrical shock.

O'Brien moves quickly, warning Flith and Bilby not to do anything — Krole has been "spiked" — and shuts down the shocks from the panel (easily, given that he trapped it in the first place). He uses this as Evidence — proof that he

*knows his way around high-tech equipment — and takes the Advantage "Undercover as a Fix-it Man". Krole discovers that his dataport has fused, and is worried about asking for a replacement from the Syndicate, but O'Brien uses this as an opportunity to push himself in deeper, offering to repair the device, but for a price. This is a Persuade Task, with O'Brien using his **Presence + Engineering** (success is a matter of making an impression, and his ability to fix things), using the Advantage he'd just created to open this opportunity. O'Brien's only asked for payment, rather than an invitation to join, so the Gamemaster sets the Difficulty at 1, and O'Brien buys a die by adding to Threat to push things a little further in his favor. He succeeds, and Bilby is convinced. O'Brien says he'll have the dataport repaired and polished by tomorrow morning.*

O'Brien has overcome the obstacle "become known to the Syndicate", and now has a way in. He can build trust and usefulness in subsequent scenes.

EXTENDED TASKS IN SOCIAL CONFLICTS

Another natural way to expand a Social Conflict is by using Extended Tasks. This is a little trickier than using a Challenge, as Extended Tasks work best when there is a significant underlying risk, peril, or tension in a scene. Extended Tasks add to the tension by making it uncertain how quickly a situation can be resolved.

So long as the situation has ample tension — a race against time, or escalating risk with every passing moment — an Extended Task is best used to expand an attempt to deceive or intimidate someone. In these contexts, the effects of the social tool do not take effect until the Extended Task has been completed.

This adds emphasis to the social tools and, used in isolation, this means that the situation is probably something that should be resolved by a single successful Persuade Task, something impossible without the social tool.

Creating an Extended Task for this purpose is relatively straightforward, as the target character's Attributes,

Disciplines, and Focuses can all be used as a baseline. In each case, the Extended Task has a Magnitude of 1 for Minor NPCs, a Magnitude of 3 for Notable NPCs, and a Magnitude of 5 for Major NPCs. In either case, the base Difficulty for Tasks to complete these Extended Tasks should be determined as normal for the social tool in question.

Deception: When creating an Extended Task for deception, the Work track should equal the target's Reason or Insight, plus either their Command or Science, using whichever is highest. If the character has any Focuses applicable to spotting deceit, they gain Resistance equal to whichever Discipline they are using.

Intimidation: When creating an Extended Task for intimidation, the Work track should equal the target's Control or Presence, plus either their Command or Security, using whichever is highest. If the character has any Focuses applicable to resisting coercion, they gain Resistance equal to whichever Discipline they are using. Alternatively, see the sidebar *Social Tools in Combat*.

Negotiation: Negotiation is not well-suited to Extended Tasks, as it is resolved more through offers and counter-offers than through Tasks.

Evidence: Evidence is not normally suited to Extended Tasks, as presenting evidence does not inherently require any Tasks.

Example: *Continuing with Chief O'Brien's infiltration of the Orion Syndicate, O'Brien (using the alias of "Connelly") has begun working for the Syndicate, and has repaired a case of defective Klingon disruptors at Bilby's request. So far, O'Brien has overcome two obstacles: "become known to the Syndicate", and "be invited to join the Syndicate", but not gained the full access he needs.*

O'Brien presents the disruptors to Bilby, but the Gamemaster spends some Threat to keep the pressure on, and Flith asks where "Connelly" got the parts, as they're not easy to come by locally. O'Brien got the replacement parts from his Starfleet Intelligence contact, so he'll need to come up with another explanation. The Gamemaster sets up an Extended Task for the Deception, using Bilby's Attributes and Disciplines: Work

SOCIAL TOOLS IN COMBAT

While not really a place for nuanced debate, combat does not preclude social conflict. A significant part of battle can be the morale of the combatants, and learning how to influence or dishearten an enemy can be a vital part of a fight.

INTIMIDATION
Warning shots, suppressive fire, battle cries (Klingons always like an air of ferocity) shock tactics and other methods can be used to demoralize an enemy. The method used may cause the combination of Attribute and Discipline to vary: a well-timed warning shot is likely to be **Control + Security**, the same as an attack; a battle cry could be **Presence + Security** or **Presence + Command**. The result will be the same roll a number of ⚔ equal to 2+ the Discipline used, and apply that as damage, reducing the target's Stress as if they had been successfully attacked. However, this damage cannot cause an Injury. If five or more damage is inflicted, after Resistance, or if the target is reduced to 0 Stress, then that target is demoralized. This counts as a Complication on all further actions taken for the remainder of the fight. An ally or superior officer may be able to remove the Complication; being demoralized also allows for a Persuade Task to compel demoralized characters to surrender.

Note however, that different cultures have different responses to threats. Vulcans cannot be scared, although they can be compelled to see the logic of surrender given sufficient evidence. Klingons regards fear as something shameful, and may be executed in the field for cowardice. Superiors or ambitious subordinates can execute

cowards, and this is an expected part of Klingon military conduct. Wily foes, like Cardassians and Romulans, may retreat from battle while planning a trap or counter-attack. Some foes cannot be demoralized at all (as shown by their Immune to Fear ability). Borg drones are emotionless, while Jem'Hadar already consider themselves dead and fight to earn their lives, along with their next dose of ketracel-white.

DECEPTION
Knowledge is power, and ensuring that the enemy in battle knows less or has the facts wrong can be vital to success.

Deception provides new context to actions that affects how a target acts and makes decisions. In a Social Conflict, this is to create new possibilities in a Persuade Task: for example, a Cardassian prison guard is more likely to let a Bajoran enter if he thinks she's a comfort woman for the prison's Intendant, a tactic used frequently during the occupation of Bajor. In combat, deception can influence the enemy leader's plans, creating openings and opportunities that might otherwise not exist.

There are two factors in battlefield deception: the lie, and the medium:

- **The lie** is misinformation that the Player Characters want the enemy to believe, and the outcome they expect.

12, Resistance 3, with a Magnitude of 3. The Gamemaster says that he'll add two points to Threat for every Task attempted for this — the Syndicate's suspicions will grow the longer it takes to get a satisfactory answer.

O'Brien first tries to dismiss the suspicion, succeeding only barely, and marking off only one points on the Work track. Flith and Bilby both press O'Brien for details of his source, saying that they might need something else later. O'Brien claims that his supplier would rather remain anonymous, succeeding well enough to mark off five more on the Work track and get a Breakthrough, but he's not safe yet. The Gamemaster spends three more Threat, and Bilby gets angry, pressing O'Brien for an answer. The Gamemaster says that unless O'Brien can complete the Extended Task with the next test, there'll be trouble.

O'Brien struggles for a moment, then comes up with an answer. He goes all-in, adding to Threat to buy additional dice in the hope that it'll work, and makes the claim that he stole the parts, and didn't want to tell so that Bilby couldn't be implicated if he got caught. Succeeding spectacularly, O'Brien fills the rest of the Work track, scoring two Breakthroughs in the process. Bilby is so impressed with

"Connelly's" loyalty that the following Persuade Task — which would have represented O'Brien attempting to gain the Syndicate's trust — is reduced to Difficulty 0.

OPPOSING ACTIONS

During a Social Conflict scene, the target is unlikely to just sit while events unfold. As well as the Gamemaster roleplaying decisions and responses, and rolling for Opposed Tasks, there's room for NPCs to fight back.

In some situations, each side will be pursuing their own, possibly exclusive, goals and attempting Tasks towards them independently. That won't always be the case, and it is useful to consider the kinds of actions that a character in Social Conflict may attempt when she doesn't have any immediate goals.

The options here are the Social Tools. The target of a Social Conflict may not have immediate goals of their own, but they could figure out their opponents' goals and react accordingly. Perhaps they try to gain some benefit from the situation by negotiating; perhaps they meet intimidation with threats and taunts of their own; or perhaps they dissemble and give false information. Any of these options could easily create

Good examples of this are a false retreat from a fight to lure an enemy into a trap, or convincing an enemy that reinforcements are coming to redirect their attention.

An iconic example is Kirk's deception about the Corbomite Device, convincing the Romulans that destroying the Enterprise will lead to their own deaths.

- **The medium** is how the Player Characters intend to get the lie to the target. In battle, simply talking to the enemy isn't usually an option, as they are likely to expect deception. Instead, the lie needs to be conveyed through action, and that may be the tricky bit, particularly with more complex lies.

To continue the Kirk example above, he used channels the Romulans were known to have cracked (although the Romulans didn't know this had been discovered by Starfleet) allowed him to communicate the lie without rousing their suspicion, as they assumed he was telling the truth to his superiors, not lying to them.

Once both the lie and the medium have been determined, the most senior (or most appropriate) Player Character involved must make a **Control** or **Daring + Command** or **Security Task**, opposed by the enemy leader making an **Insight** or **Reason + Command** or **Security Task**. Success

means that the enemy believes the lie, and will respond to the misinformation accordingly. Complications may mean the enemy believes the lie, but responds in an unexpected "wrong" manner, or have suspicions that not everything is as it seems. Failure means that the enemy sees through the deception.

NEGOTIATION AND EVIDENCE

There's normally less opportunity for these social tools in the noise and mess of battle. It can be easier during ship-to-ship combat, where commanders can hail one another and talk during lulls in the fighting.

Negotiation is most commonly used as a call to end any fighting, offering concessions (temporary or long-lasting) to an opponent to convince them to yield, or asking for something in exchange for a surrender.

Evidence may be vital in defusing a conflict if the fighting started because of a misunderstanding, though this is likely to require work (and a Task) to convince the enemy that any evidence is real. Alternately, signs of reinforcements arriving may be considered evidence that an enemy should withdraw, as was the case when Sisko convinced Gowron to end his attack on Deep Space 9 (*Deep Space Nine*, "The Way of the Warrior").

In either case, there are no changes or additional considerations to using these methods in combat, as long as the characters can communicate with one another.

Advantages in the character's favor, make things easier for them, or harder for their opponents.

Of course, if a Social Conflict target is aggressive or easily provoked they may attack, changing the nature of the scene entirely. This option should be used sparingly, perhaps as a Threat spend (2 Threat is a reasonable cost) during a particularly tense scene.

PUTTING IT ALL TOGETHER

With the core rulebook tools in mind, and supported by the additional material here, this section looks at some Social Conflict scenes, and provides suggestions on putting these ideas into practice:

Cold War Ceasefire: Two mutually hostile forces are arrayed against each other but are not yet in open conflict. There may be some manner of treaty that holds war at bay but tensions are high, and the situation has escalated things to a point where fighting could break out shortly. Neither side wants war, but neither is willing to simply back down. The key here is a mixture of showing strength (weakness may encourage the other side to get what they want through force) and making concessions (a mixture of intimidation and negotiation, possibly with deception and/or evidence depending on what proof of intent can be shown). The basic Persuade Task should revolve around everyone leaving without a fight, but this should be impossible without everyone giving something up in exchange; giving something up too easily may display weakness.

The Gamemaster should ramp up the pressure, making the situation timed or by adding one or two points to Threat with each exchange (every Task or other instance of a social tool and its response). Remember that the enemy has a goal and will act to achieve it: they want an ending without a fight, but they can't back down without gaining something. This is ideally suited to situations involving the Klingons (*Enterprise* and the Original Series eras), the Romulans (any era), the Cardassians (*The Next Generation* era, especially before

the Cardassian Demilitarized Zone is established), or the Dominion (any time before the Dominion War).

Infiltration: Infiltrating a hostile force often requires considerable preparation, and comes with considerable risks to the infiltrators if they are discovered. The force being infiltrated is largely passive and, if all goes well, the organization won't even know what's happening, and will act if suspicions are aroused. Deception is crucial, supported by falsified evidence (surgical alterations and other disguises, fake identities, etc.), but must be done carefully. Unless the Player Characters keep things straightforward, the Gamemaster is encouraged to increase the Complication range as the lies grow in number and complexity. Negotiations can be useful for gaining leverage and expanding connections, while intimidation can be useful for maintaining an appearance of strength. Infiltration is perilous, and failures can lead to suspicion, discovery, and retaliation. Infiltration is often used with criminal and clandestine organizations like the Orion Syndicate, smuggling rings, and the Maquis (*The Next Generation* era), but also to obtain secrets from or sabotage the efforts of hostile nations (this normally requires surgery to pose as another species).

Interrogation: This is normally part of a criminal investigation or when dealing with prisoners of war. In these situations, one or two interrogators (though others may be observing nearby) question a single subject. There may be multiple suspects or captives, but they should be interrogated one at a time rather than together. The interrogators have one goal: obtaining vital information that the subject knows, while the subject's only objective is to avoid revealing any information although this may change to self-preservation. The subject will probably start by flat-out refusing to comply, but may switch to other methods (deception or intimidation) to hinder the interrogators. The subject may negotiate to gain something in exchange for what they know (in criminal investigations, this is often immunity from prosecution). The interrogators will use evidence to try and convince the subject that the situation is hopeless, along with intimidation (threats of future punishment and incarceration), deception (claiming that other subjects have confessed, for example), and negotiation (compliance brings rewards or lesser punishment).

Legal Proceedings: Courts-martial and other hearings are occasionally necessary in Starfleet. Command officers are therefore expected to have a basic familiarity with courtroom protocol and procedures. Legal proceedings typically have two active participants: the prosecution or plaintiff, and the defense (or their representatives), who take turns arguing their case using whatever evidence and rhetorical techniques they like to present their version of the truth. There will also be numerous passive participants, including an array of witnesses and experts giving testimony (providing evidence), a judge or adjudicator (who enforces the court's rules and makes certain decisions), and a jury/group (who will come to a verdict, although this might be the judge's role). In

I have ordered the *U.S.S. Oldfield* to begin first contact procedures with the Sluarilians, due to the incident on stardate 42432. Their instructions are strict: to make first contact, with the team of purely Denobulan crew, confirming their existence as alien beings. They are not to disclose other alien species, but only that they are part of a wider Federation of worlds. They are not to interfere any further in the Sluarilians' development, in strict keeping of the Prime Directive.

My hope is this intervention will mean the Sluarilians continue onward with their observed policy of space exploration, leading to full first contact once warp capability is reached. I'm ordering a scientific survey team to establish an outpost in the system to monitor the Sluarilians with long-range sensor equipment to minimize the threat of contaminating any further development of the Sluarilian civilization.

We've already made mistakes; best rectify them now before the Sluarilian population destroys itself over 'flying saucer' rumors.

— Admiral Wakenshaw, Starbase 174, Sectors 21166-23079

broad terms, the prosecution or plaintiff have something they wish proved, and they must convince the jury about their case; the defense must persuade the jury to the contrary, or introduce reasonable doubt. The prosecution goes first, question each witness, and allowing the defense questions, repeating until all witnesses have been heard. The defense then introduce their witnesses and evidence. Legal proceedings are often prolonged affairs, although individual witnesses and their testimony, may take only a short time.

Use of social tools other than evidence is tricky in court. A judge is likely to respond negatively to other methods especially if they're overt, but they might be useful during pre-trial periods to convince witnesses to testify.

Peace Negotiations: These can require considerable care and tact. Two warring factions, still holding grudges, but both acknowledging that the war cannot continue must be brought together. The causes of war are probably still present as the warring parties haven't managed to end the central conflict, but there is a chance for peace. Perhaps there is a lull in the fighting, or a third party has intervened. Both sides have a common goal of peace but both also want something else, the "something" that caused the war in the first place. Resolving that issue may be extremely difficult at best. Neither side trusts the other and, while nobody wants the war to continue, they will fight if pushed.

Peace negotiations are likely to be long-winded, covering many related issues that need to be resolved before any final peace agreement. They are normally handled by diplomats and negotiators, but starship crews provide a venue (the ship) and some personnel to assist proceedings, or carry delegates to a suitably neutral meeting place. Threats and intimidation are likely to be of short-term benefit, while deception can be particularly perilous because it could escalate tensions if a lie is detected.

Instead, the peace process requires openness and honesty, so evidence and negotiation are the most valuable social tools in this situation.

Trade Deals: Trade deals are similar to peace negotiations, but not as tense. The talks will typically involve two parties: sellers and buyers. The valuable goods could be anything: a physical resource or scarce material; access to a trade route; a manufacturing process that is unknown elsewhere; technology; settlement rights on a particular world; or even an ongoing general trading relationship. The seller obviously wishes to make the greatest gains possible, while the buyer wants to pay the lowest possible cost. The difference between those goals is where the Social Conflict is found.

Negotiation is the heart of a trade deal, with each party offering prices, quantities, profit percentages, contract durations, and any other variations on a deal as a way to reach agreement. Evidence is similarly useful: a demonstration of the valuables' high worth; extensive financial projections that illustrate costs and profits; and other proof that allows each party to trust the other.

Threats are likely to sour trade talks, unless they are carefully presented (such as a threat to trade with a competitor), and even those risk bringing proceedings to a halt. Similarly, lies need to be used delicately, to embellish the worth of something or to introduce innocuous-seeming terms and conditions (clauses commonly known as "Ferengi-print"). These can be extremely lucrative for one party and costly to the other, but such practices tend to be poorly regarded and give a merchant a bad reputation.

Trade negotiations aren't normally the responsibility of Starfleet officers, but they may be called to arbitrate, provide a venue, or send personnel to support the negotiations, act as security or generally show the flag.

USING THE COMMAND DIVISION
STARBASES

STARBASE MECHANICS

As discussed in the **Star Trek Adventures** *core rulebook*, a posting on a starbase is similar to life aboard a starship. The biggest difference is that a starbase tends to build close ties to a local community, becomes a key part of local civilian life and regional trade, and accommodates families and other non-Starfleet inhabitants. In game terms, a starbase is essentially a large immobile starship. Most starbase designs are significantly larger than even *Galaxy*-class starships. Starbases have a limited capacity to adjust their position and orientation but moving a starbase any significant distance is not done lightly.

STARBASE DATA

Starbases, like starships, are represented using a mixture of Traits, Systems, Departments, and Talents, and each starbase will have an **operations center** which serves much the same role as a ship's bridge. In the broadest terms, whenever a character performs a Task that makes use of a starbase's systems and functions, the starbase itself provides assistance in the same manner as a starship.

- **TRAITS:** A starbase will typically have at least one Trait, which will always include the name of the civilization that created it. Starbase 375 has the Trait *Federation Starbase*, while Deep Space 9 has the trait *Cardassian Mining Station*. A starbase may also have a Trait reflecting its current allegiance, if that differs from the creators. Deep Space 9 may be Cardassian in design, but it is *Federation-run, Bajoran-owned*. A starbase may also have a Trait showing its purpose or importance. Deep Space 9 is the *Station at the mouth of the Wormhole*.

- **SYSTEMS:** A starbase has the six starship Systems of Communications, Computers, Engines, Sensors, Structure, and Weapons. It is likely to have a score above 12 in these, thanks to its size and lack of propulsion spaces. A starbase's Engines score does not represent propulsion systems, but rather the station's reactors.

- **DEPARTMENT:** A starbase has the usual six Departments of Command, Conn, Engineering, Security, Science, and Medicine, but these are likely to have higher scores than a starship. A starbase's facilities tend to be rather more extensive than any in a ship. A starbase's Conn score covers flight crews and maintenance personnel for its many shuttles and small craft, rather than flight control systems for the starbase.

- **TALENTS:** Starbases have Talents, just as characters and starships do. They can take any Starship Talents, but not ones that affect how starship moves. A starbase can have a number of Talents equal to half (rounding down) its Scale.

- **SCALE:** A starbase has a scale just like a starship. Many starbases have a Scale much higher than that of a starship: 10, 12, or even more (in the case of stations such as Earth Spacedock).

- **RESISTANCE:** Starbases have a Resistance score that is determined exactly as a starship's Resistance — it is equal to the station's Scale.

- **SHIELDS:** A starbase's Shields are equal to its Structure plus its Security, just like a starship.

- **POWER:** A starbase has a base Power capacity equal to its Engines score.

- **CREW SUPPORT:** A starbase has Crew Support per mission equal to Scale. As a Starbase often has civilian inhabitants as well as Starfleet personnel, players may use Crew Support to create civilian or Starfleet Supporting Characters. When first created, a civilian Supporting Character may reduce any one Discipline by 1, to a minimum of 0, to increase one other Discipline.

- **SMALL CRAFT:** A starbase can support a number of active small craft equal to its Scale minus 1 at any time, just like a starship. Starbases may always support runabouts and other Scale 2 small craft (they count as two craft towards the limit, as usual), even without the Extensive Shuttlebay talent.

OPERATIONS: A starbase has an operations center or "Ops," which provides access to all the control systems and consoles necessary to keep the station working. It is similar to a starship's bridge, and can be designed in the same way, although a starbase doesn't have Helm or Navigator positions. The Commanding Officer's office is normally adjacent to Ops.

DOCKING STARSHIPS

Large starbases allow for repairs, maintenance and resupply of starships. While transporters allow a vessel to transfer personnel and cargo near-instantly, docking allows a ship to power down its systems. Thorough diagnostics and repairs can be performed which could not be done otherwise.

A starbase with a Scale of 9 or higher has a number of docking ports equal to half its Scale, rounding down. Each docking port can support a single vessel of no greater than half the Station's Scale (rounding down). For example, a Scale 10 station has 5 docking ports, each of which can support Scale 5 (or less) vessels. The Docking Capacity talent can expand this capability.

A docked vessel does not generate Power, and cannot be used for any Starship Task. Life support and internal communications are operational and are connected to those of the station. A docked vessel's shields are always considered down, though they cannot be targeted independently while any station's shields are operational; docked ships are within the station's shields.

STARBASE TALENTS

DOCKING CAPACITY

The station has additional ports and pylons that allow it to support a greater number of docked vessels as well as larger vessels than would normally be the case. The starbase has a number of docking ports equal to one-and-a-half times its Scale (rounding down), instead of half its Scale. The maximum Scale of any ship that may dock at the station is increased by 2.

ENHANCED DEFENSE GRID

The station's Shields are increased by an amount equal to half the station's Scale.

FIREBASE

The station is built to defend itself and surrounding space from attack and can unleash colossal firepower. Whenever a character makes an Attack with the station, they may use the Swift Task Momentum Spend for 1 Momentum instead of the normal 2, so long as their second Task is also an Attack.

REPAIR CREWS

With additional personnel to support repair and maintenance work, the station may prioritize repairs to a number of ships equal to its Engineering Department.

STURDY CONSTRUCTION

When the station suffers damage, after Resistance, from an attack or hazard, it suffers a Breach if 8 or more damage is inflicted, rather than 5 or more as is normally the case.

A vessel docked at a starbase can be repaired. A single Breach per day the ship is docked can be repaired. Extra days equal to the ship's Scale are needed for each system that was Destroyed. A character may direct a repair team to prioritize a particular ship's repairs (only one ship may be prioritized in this way at any given time), requiring a **Presence + Command** or **Presence + Engineering Task** with a Difficulty of 2. Success removes 2 days from the total repair time, plus an additional day per Momentum spent (Repeatable). Each Complication may add 2 days to repairs, thanks to component shortages and similar logistical problems. The Gamemaster may increase the Difficulty and Complication Range of this Task based on the availability of parts and personnel to perform the repairs. A Starbase may repair its own Breaches at the same rate.

EXAMPLE STARBASES

The following starbase types are found throughout the Federation.

SMALL DEEP SPACE OUTPOST

These compact facilities are used as listening posts and border stations, and have a relatively small crew by starbase standards. Their crews use large numbers of small craft to scout the surrounding area and support any nearby starships missions . The outposts are normally too far from settled star systems to be important to local commerce and politics, and an assignment one is much like a starship assignment in many ways.

TRAITS: Federation Starbase

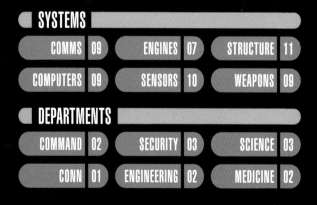

SYSTEMS

| COMMS | 09 | ENGINES | 07 | STRUCTURE | 11 |
| COMPUTERS | 09 | SENSORS | 10 | WEAPONS | 09 |

DEPARTMENTS

| COMMAND | 02 | SECURITY | 03 | SCIENCE | 03 |
| CONN | 01 | ENGINEERING | 02 | MEDICINE | 02 |

POWER: 7   **SCALE:** 8
SHIELDS: 19   **RESISTANCE:** 8

CREW SUPPORT: 8

DOCKING CAPACITY: Up to 4 vessels, each of Scale 4 or less.

ATTACKS:

- Phaser Arrays (Range Medium, 11▲ damage, Versatile 2, Area or Spread)
- Photon Torpedoes (Range Long, 6▲, High Yield)

TALENTS

- Advanced Sensor Suites
- Advanced Shields (included above)
- Extensive Shuttlebays
- Rugged Design

FRONT LINE STARBASE

These large starbases are found in areas of military, economic, or political importance. As such areas tend to have important, populated worlds these starbases often influence local politics, commerce and defense. Their crews often have family on board, as starbase assignments have a long-term stability missing from life on a starship.

TRAITS: Federation Starbase

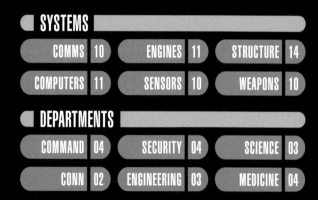

SYSTEMS

| COMMS | 10 | ENGINES | 11 | STRUCTURE | 14 |
| COMPUTERS | 11 | SENSORS | 10 | WEAPONS | 10 |

DEPARTMENTS

| COMMAND | 04 | SECURITY | 04 | SCIENCE | 03 |
| CONN | 02 | ENGINEERING | 03 | MEDICINE | 04 |

POWER: 11   **SCALE:** 10
SHIELDS: 18   **RESISTANCE:** 10

CREW SUPPORT: 10

DOCKING CAPACITY: Up to 15 vessels, each of Scale 7 or less.

ATTACKS:

- Phaser Arrays (Range Medium, 14▲, Versatile 2, Area or Spread)
- Photon Torpedoes (Range Long, 7▲, High Yield)

TALENTS

- Docking Capacity (included above)
- Advanced Sickbay
- Repair Crews
- Sturdy Construction
- Rapid-Fire Torpedo Launcher

AWARDS AND COMMENDATIONS

RENOWN

An officer's renown and reputation are important. Respected officers will get better assignments, prestigious missions, and be consulted by superior officers for their expertise. They often have a freedom of action that might see other officers disciplined — as long as those actions are necessary.

Renown is often accompanied by awards and commendations, with each award marking some praiseworthy or significant event in the officer's career. These awards are applicable to personnel regardless of their rank, division, or department, and many officers accrue awards throughout their careers. Physical medals are normally only worn with dress uniforms or kept in a display case.

AWARDS

Whenever a character's Reputation increases, they may receive an award which costs a certain amount of gained Reputation. Each award has a lasting impact, and grants the character bonuses. A character may only earn a single Award from any given mission.

Each of the Awards below has a listed Reputation cost, which a character can spend to earn that Award. In effect, the character exchanges a quantity of abstract Reputation for a specific benefit. A character may only spend Reputation that they have just earned as a result of a completed mission. Reputation earned in previous missions cannot be spent on Awards, and they may also have conditions that must be met during a mission, such as the performance of a particular act or feat. The Gamemaster's discretion applies in determining if a condition is met.

Each Award gives a benefit, which is applied permanently to the character. Even if the character's Reputation later falls, they still possess the Award.

CHRISTOPHER PIKE MEDAL OF VALOR

A prestigious medal awarded to Starfleet officers in recognition of remarkable leadership, meritorious conduct, and acts of personal bravery. It is named for legendary Starfleet officer Christopher Pike.

COST: 4

CONDITIONS: The character must be an officer in a command or leadership position who has led their crew in a succession of several difficult missions, and faced personal danger on at least two of those missions.

BENEFIT: Once per mission when the character uses the Direct Task, instead of rolling normally they may treat their d20 as if it had rolled a 1.

COCHRANE MEDAL OF EXCELLENCE

The Cochrane Medal of Excellence is awarded by the Zefram Cochrane Institute for Advanced Theoretical Physics to Starfleet officers and cadets who perform outstanding feats in the fields of science and engineering.

COST: 3

CONDITIONS: The character must have significantly contributed to a field of scientific study or engineering. Making and documenting an important discovery or finding a solution to a long-standing problem would be typical achievements.

BENEFIT: Select a single Focus the character possesses that relates to the scientific or engineering field for which they earned the award. Once per mission, when the character spends a point of Determination on a Task that involves that Focus, they receive two of the benefits of spending a point of Determination instead of one.

CONDITIONS: The character must have faced extreme
danger and overwhelming odds in combat or a similar crisis
and survived, and also succeeded in defending a Federation
world or outpost from loss or destruction.

BENEFIT: Once per mission, when the character would
suffer an Injury, the character may Avoid the Injury for free.
Alternatively, once per mission when the character's ship
would suffer one or more Breaches, they may either spend
2 Momentum (Immediate) or suffer a Complication to ignore
one of those Breaches. Only one Order benefit may apply in
any single mission.

LEGION OF HONOR

The Legion of Honor is a commendation for Starfleet
personnel who act in a way that exemplifies the very best
qualities of Starfleet.

COST: 4

CONDITIONS: None.

BENEFIT: Once per mission the character may do one of
the following: gain two bonus Momentum on a successful
Task (bonus Momentum may not be saved); or ignore a
single Complication suffered on a Task (declared before the
Gamemaster announces the Complication's effect).

PALM LEAF OF "X" PEACE MISSION

Palm Leaves are commendations awarded to Starfleet
officers who participate in successful peace missions, such
as that to the planet Axanar in the 23rd Century. The award
contains the name of the peace mission in place of the "X"
above: for example, the Palm Leaf of Axanar.

COST: 2

CONDITIONS: The mission must have involved securing
peace between warring nations or the signing of a peace
treaty. All characters involved in the mission are eligible.

BENEFIT: Once per mission when attempting a Persuade
Task in an effort to prevent violence, the character may
reduce the Difficulty of the Persuade Task by 1, to a
minimum of 1.

STAR CROSS

The Star Cross is a medal awarded to Starfleet personnel for
distinguished actions.

COST: 3

CONDITIONS: None.

BENEFIT: Once per mission, before attempting a Task and
applying a Focus, the character may choose to double their
Focus range. For the Task, the character will score two

GRANKITE ORDER OF TACTICS

Membership of the ceremonial Grankite Order of Tactics
honors Starfleet officers who have demonstrated exceptional
tactical acumen.

COST: 3

CONDITIONS: The character must have demonstrated
exceptional skill and tactical thinking during combat or some
other crisis situation, which directly contributed to mission
success or the survival of their ship and crew.

BENEFIT: Once per mission, when the character creates an
Advantage that reflects or represents some strategy or tactic,
they may automatically create a second, identical Advantage.
They create two copies of an Advantage, to be used together
for greater effect.

KARAGITE ORDER OF HEROISM

Membership of the ceremonial Karagite Order of Heroism
is granted to Starfleet officers of exceptional heroism,
demonstrated in defense of the Federation and its people.

COST: 3

COMMENDATIONS AND THE CHAIN OF COMMAND

In many cases during the course of a mission, officers in command may find their Reputation increasing due to the actions undertaken by their subordinates. While this is to be expected because those who take the responsibility of command should be commended when their teams succeed, some officers may see this fair.

As a result, commanding officers and executive officers have the option of using their Reputation to recognize and commend their subordinates. In order to do this, the process for determining changes to Reputation is amended slightly. Characters should roll for Reputation in order of rank, starting with the highest-ranking character in the group.

If the commanding officer or executive officer gains one or more Reputation, they may choose to make a note in their log commending other main characters of lower rank, and spend some of the Reputation they have gained. Each point of "logged" Reputation spent allows one of the commended characters to roll one additional d20 on their own Reputation roll.

successes for any die that rolls equal to or less than twice their Discipline score. If, for example, the character has a Discipline score of 4, then any die that rolls an 8 or lower scores 2 Successes for that Task.

STARFLEET CITATION FOR CONSPICUOUS GALLANTRY

The Starfleet Citation for Conspicuous Gallantry is an award for an act of particular heroism by a Starfleet officer.

COST: 2

CONDITIONS: The character must have succeeded at a particularly heroic, risky, or daring action during the mission.

BENEFIT: Once per mission, when the character pays for an Immediate Momentum Spend (of any kind) by adding to Threat, they may roll 1🅐 per point of Threat added. For each Effect rolled, one of the points just added to Threat is removed immediately.

STARFLEET DECORATION OF GALLANTRY

The Starfleet Decoration of Gallantry is a medal awarded to Starfleet officers who show extreme bravery in the line of duty.

COST: 2

CONDITIONS: The character must have faced an extremely difficult or dangerous situation, and have triumphed in spite of the peril.

BENEFIT: Once per mission, whenever the character would suffer damage, halve the amount of damage inflicted by an attack or hazard.

STARFLEET MEDAL OF HONOR

The Starfleet Medal of Honor is a medal for valor presented to deserving Starfleet personnel who act above and beyond the call of duty.

COST: 5

CONDITIONS: None. It is possible to earn this medal multiple times.

BENEFIT: Once per mission, the character may gain two bonus Momentum on a successful Task (bonus Momentum may not be saved). If the character has earned this medal multiple times, then this benefit may be used once during a mission for each Medal of Honor awarded.

STARFLEET SURGEON'S DECORATION

This is a special bravery award given exclusively to Starfleet medical personnel for acts above and beyond the call of duty.

COST: 3

CONDITIONS: The character must be a Medical officer of some kind, and must go above and beyond the call of duty in an attempt to save a patient, or otherwise alleviate some medical crisis.

BENEFIT: Once per mission, the character may reduce the Difficulty of a single Medical Task by 1, to a minimum of 1.

USING THE COMMAND DIVISION
FLEET ENGAGEMENTS

ESTABLISHING SCALE

There are times when a single vessel is not enough to complete a particular objective, and these times make necessary fleet actions requiring many ships. Fleet actions are a simpler way to resolve the actions of a large number of ships, individually or in groups. This is normally done for large-scale combat, but it can handle any activity involving large numbers of vessels.

When establishing a fleet action the Gamemaster must determine the size of the action, in terms of the number and type of ships involved on each side. This information is the basis for everything that follows.

FLEET STRENGTH

A fleet's total strength is a factor of the number and type of ships involved. In a fleet each vessel has a strength equal to its Scale. Each ship should be created by combining a Class and a Mission Profile, but it isn't necessary to consider Refits or Talents for ships being created specifically for a fleet action. Those details aren't important. The strength of all the ships in the fleet added together is the total fleet strength.

At this point the total number of ships should be considered. If there are more than six ships in a fleet, they may be grouped into wings which will act together. Some thought should be given to how groups are formed, because groups of similar vessels can capitalize on shared strengths. Some vessels may be more when not grouped in a wing.

Wing grouping does not have to result in equal numbers in each wing, but it may be useful if each group has roughly the same total strength where ships vary in size. For example, a group of Fighters (three Scale 2 small craft) forms one wing; another is a single *Galaxy*-class starship (a Scale 6 vessel).

FLEET ACTIONS

Regardless of the number of ships in a group it receives a single Turn, and each Turn consists of two Actions. Turns are taken in the same way as with any Conflict, with sides alternating and having the option to pay to Keep the Initiative.

Actions can be chosen from the following list, and each action can be taken more than once:

- **ADVANCE:** The vessel or group moves two zones.

- **ATTACK RUN:** The vessel or group moves one zone and makes an attack. The target may be a vessel or group in the same or an adjacent zone.

- **DIRECT:** May only be attempted by a vessel with a Command of 4 or more, or by a group containing a vessel with Command 4+. One other vessel or group within Long range receives one additional Action, which may be taken immediately.

- **DISENGAGE:** The vessel or group moves one zone. The vessel or group's defense increases by +2 until the start of their next turn.

- **FEINT:** The vessel or group moves one zone, and prepares to attack a vessel or group in the same zone or an adjacent one. No attack is made, but the targeted enemy counts as having defended two additional attacks this round.

- **FLANK SPEED:** The vessel or group moves three zones; however, it counts its defense as two lower than normal until the start of its next Turn.

- **REGROUP:** If *damaged*, the vessel or group moves one zone, and then regroups (see below).

- **WORK:** The vessel or group moves one zone, and then carries out some activity. This has no specific effects but such an action may be necessary depending on the situation and the mission.

Any vessel that has a Conn of 4+, or any group which consists entirely of vessels with Conn 4+, may move one additional zone as part of its move. Groups that consist entirely of Small Craft also gain this benefit, regardless of their Conn score.

ATTACKING AND DEFENDING

Each vessel or group has a pair of derived scores: attack and defense. These scores are equal to the strength of all the vessels in that group, added together.

When a vessel or group makes an attack, roll a number of Challenge Dice equal to the attack of attacking group or vessel. This is the total attack strength.

The defender then rolls ⚔ equal to the defense of the defending group or vessel. This is the total defense strength.

Each subsequent time a vessel or group attacks during a single round reduce its attack by 1, to a minimum of 0. Each subsequent time a vessel or group defends during a round, reduce its defense by 1, to a minimum of 0.

Any vessel that has a Security of 4+, or any group consisting entirely of vessels with Security 4+ may add +1 for each Effect rolled.

If both totals are equal then nothing further happens. If one side's total is higher, then the other side becomes *damaged*. If they are already *damaged*, then they are

instead *destroyed*. A *damaged* group or vessel can only take a single action each Turn. A *destroyed* group or vessel takes no further part in the battle, as ships are crippled, abandoned, or destroyed outright.

A *damaged* group or vessel may spend an action to Regroup (as noted above). If it regroups, roll ⚔ equal to the group or vessel's defense, adding +1 for each Effect if

FASTER RESOLUTION

Especially large fleet actions can require the rolling of a lot Challenge Dice. This could slow things down while fistfuls of dice are rolled and their results totaled. Additionally, the Gamemaster may wish to resolve large fleet battles quickly as a backdrop to other events.

Whenever a large number of Challenge Dice would need to be rolled, the Gamemaster may instead choose to determine the average, and use that instead.

To complete this relatively quickly, split the Challenge Dice into groups of six. For every 6⚔, the total is 5. If some rule grants +1 to the total per Effect rolled the total is 7. If there are any Challenge Dice remaining that don't fit into a full group of six, roll those Challenge Dice as normal.

regrouping vessels are within the same zone as a ship with an Engineering or Medicine of 4+. This supporting ship may be in the same group, or a different one: repair crews, medical personnel, and casualties can be beamed between vessels as required. If the total rolled is equal to or greater than the group or vessel's strength, then it immediately stops being *damaged*.

PLAYER CHARACTERS AND FLEET ACTIONS

Fleet actions do not involve ordinary Tasks or the activities of Player Characters. However, it is highly likely that several Player Characters could be involved in a fleet action, either on a single ship or spread across several groups.

Single Ship: The Player Characters operate their usual vessel. The fleet action is resolved in the background, with the Players' ship as an individual vessel on one side. At various points through the scene and at the Gamemaster's discretion, the action switches to a single normal combat round with the Players' ship and whatever enemy they are currently fighting. The fleet action is the backdrop to the Player Characters' heroics, rather than involving the Player Characters directly.

Several Ships: The Player Characters are spread across several vessels. Whenever a group containing a Player Character takes its turn, the Player Character may attempt a single Task before the group takes any actions, with a Difficulty of 3. Success grants the group one of the following:

- One Extra Action

- Reroll any number of dice for attack or defense once before the group's next turn.

- Add 1▲, plus an additional ▲ for each Momentum spent, to the group's attack or defense once before the group's next turn.

- Move one additional zone whenever the group moves this turn.

- Automatically allow regrouping without rolling.

Depending on the nature of the Task attempted, the Gamemaster may allow other benefits.

CHAPTER 06.00

COMMAND PERSONNEL

25657347457
68356823124122221

COMMAND PERSONNEL
STARFLEET COMMAND

"HERE, IN THE DELTA QUADRANT, WE ARE VIRTUALLY THE ENTIRE FAMILY OF MAN. WE ARE MORE THAN A CREW, AND I MUST FIND A WAY TO BE MORE THAN A CAPTAIN TO THESE PEOPLE."

— CAPTAIN KATHRYN JANEWAY

OVERVIEW

During their voyages and missions the crew of a starship will inevitably encounter Starfleet Command personnel: admirals, specialists, advisors, and senior staff are part of Starfleet life, even on the frontier. This section presents several such characters that Gamemasters can use in campaigns and missions.

COMMODORE ROBERT APRIL [MAJOR NPC]

Commodore April is perhaps best known because he is part of a small group of officers who captained the *Enterprise*. As commander of the San Francisco Naval Yards in the 2240s, April oversaw the development of the *Constitution*-class starships, including the hull that would become the *Enterprise*. He then took command of the *Enterprise* for its initial missions from 2245 onwards.

After 5 years in the captain's chair, April was promoted to commodore and created as Ambassador-at-Large, representing Federation interests across numerous worlds. He was accompanied by his wife, the noted physician Doctor Sarah April, who had been his chief medical officer on the *Enterprise*. He was due to retire from active service in 2270, but this has been indefinitely postponed.

Like the men who followed him on the *Enterprise*, April is headstrong and bold, unafraid of personal risk, but also deeply compassionate. His age and experience have tempered his audacity, but he is nevertheless a man who desires action and activity, and one who has little tolerance for suffering inflicted on others.

VALUES:
- A Ship is a Home, and its Crew is a Family
- No Regrets for a Life Lived Well
- To Explore Strange New Worlds...
- Compelled to Ease the Plight of Others

TRAITS: Human, Flag Officer

ATTRIBUTES

CONTROL	09	FITNESS	08	PRESENCE	10
DARING	11	INSIGHT	10	REASON	09

DISCIPLINES

COMMAND	05	SECURITY	03	SCIENCE	03
CONN	02	ENGINEERING	03	MEDICINE	01

FOCUSES: Diplomacy, Inspiration, Politics, Starship Design, Starship Tactics, Willpower

STRESS: 11   **RESISTANCE:** 0

ATTACKS:
- Unarmed Strike (Melee, 4⬣ Knockdown, Size 1H, Non-Lethal)
- Phaser Type-1 (Ranged, 5⬣, Size 1H, Charge, Hidden 1)

SPECIAL RULES:
- **Audacious Commander:** When attempting a command Task, and spending one or more points of Threat to buy additional dice, he may re-roll a single d20.
- **Renowned:** When a mission concludes under his command, or where he was involved , each Player Character may re-roll a single d20 on their Reputation roll.
- **Lead by Doing:** Whenever a point of Determination is spent on a Directive which was one of his Values, roll 1⬣. On an Effect, that point of Determination is not spent.

REAR ADMIRAL TORTHEM JAV BRIN [MAJOR NPC]

Admiral Brin is an acerbic and driven individual currently commanding a research and exploratory fleet on the edges of the Federation. She expects only the best from the officers in her command, and sets an even higher standard for herself. Brin embraces the politics of her station, but her meticulous and piercing insight means that few are inclined to play politics with her. Instead, she makes do with a good battle of words, and frequently engages the captains under her command in debate. Brin is given considerable leeway to run her fleet as she sees fit.

She is quick to criticize flaws, but just as quick to offer praise for a job well done; those who know her well value her honesty and insights.

VALUES:
- A Questioning Mind is Essential for Exploration
- This Job Requires a Keen Mind and an Iron Will

TRAITS: Tellarite, Flag Officer

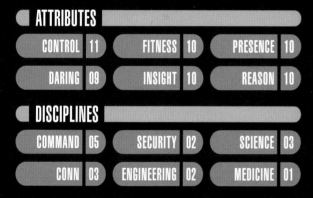

ATTRIBUTES

CONTROL	11	FITNESS	10	PRESENCE	10
DARING	09	INSIGHT	10	REASON	10

DISCIPLINES

COMMAND	05	SECURITY	02	SCIENCE	03
CONN	03	ENGINEERING	02	MEDICINE	01

FOCUSES: Astrophysics, Composure, Debate, Exoarchaeology, Politics, Psychology

STRESS: 12   **RESISTANCE:** 0

ATTACKS:
- Unarmed Strike (Melee, 3🅐 Knockdown, Size 1H, Non-lethal)
- Phaser Type-2 (Ranged, 5🅐, Size 1H, Charge)

SPECIAL RULES:
- **Shrewd Politician:** Brin's political and debating skills are considerable and few willingly engage her in a battle of words. When anyone attempts a Persuade Task against Admiral Brin, increase the Complication Range by 2, due to her ability to spot flaws in an argument.
- **Insightful Commander:** Brin is keenly observant and understands people. Once per mission, during any scene where Brin is an ally to the Player Characters, she may grant one Player Character in the same scene a point of Determination, as her advice and guidance help reassure and direct that character.
- **Menacing**

FLAG OFFICER VALUES

Each flag officer NPC has several Values, which function similar to other NPCs, adding to or removing from Threat rather than generating and spending Determination. However, in situations where a flag officer is an important part of a mission, and taking an active part, the flag officer NPC's Values can have additional importance.

At any point during a mission, a flag officer NPC may select one of their Values and add it to the list of Directives currently in play for that mission. This reflects the impact of the flag officer's beliefs and inclinations on their command style. Should this Directive be Challenged, this may change the way that the flag officer views the challenging Player Character(s), possibly creating a rival or adversary.

THREAT AND ALLIED NPCS

Many of the flag officers in this section have the Menacing or Threatening special traits. In play, a flag officer may be an ally or antagonist depending on context. It is common for admirals to get into heated debates with command officers, but they're all still Starfleet. In such situations extra thought is needed for these special abilities, given that NPC interactions with Threat vary depending on whether they are friend or foe.

MENACING

This ability adds one point to Threat when the character enters the scene. The NPC can be an ally or an adversary: always add one to Threat. This isn't always due to the character, but can reflect the circumstances that need an admiral's involvement. A flag officer taking an interest means the mission is especially important, dangerous or sensitive.

THREATENING X

This provides the character with X additional Threat to be spent exclusively by that character, rather than from the group pool. As NPCs allied to Player Characters add to Threat, rather than spending from it, there is another consideration. When a character with Threatening X is opposed to the Player Characters, points from their personal Threat pool can be spent instead of spending points from the main Threat pool. When a character with Threatening X is aligned with the Player Characters, points from the NPC's personal Threat pool can be spent instead of adding points to the main Threat pool. This reflects the character's control over a situation: flag officers are better able than most to keep a situation from escalating, or maintain a greater degree of pressure.

VICE ADMIRAL ALYNNA NECHAYEV [MAJOR NPC]

Alynna Nechayev is a senior Starfleet Admiral of considerable renown and importance in the Alpha Quadrant. In the late 2360s, she oversaw the Federation-Cardassian border, and she was instrumental in the peace treaty that led to the Cardassian Demilitarized Zone in 2370.

Her highest priority is the security of the Federation whether through peaceful negotiation, or preemptive actions such as direct strikes and covert operations. She has little patience for anything that doesn't serve that aim, and she is willing to make the tough decisions and, sometimes, concessions necessary to maintain peace and stability. Security is what matters.

VALUES:
- Our First Priority is the Lives of Federation Citizens
- Concessions Must Be Made to Ensure Our Safety
- The Maquis are a Bunch of Irresponsible Hotheads
- The Ends Justify the Means

TRAITS: Human, Flag Officer

ATTRIBUTES

| CONTROL 09 | FITNESS 08 | PRESENCE 12 |
| DARING 10 | INSIGHT 09 | REASON 10 |

DISCIPLINES

| COMMAND 05 | SECURITY 04 | SCIENCE 02 |
| CONN 02 | ENGINEERING 01 | MEDICINE 01 |

FOCUSES: Cardassian Politics, Command Procedure, Covert Operations, Diplomacy, Federation Politics, Peace Treaties

STRESS: 12   **RESISTANCE:** 0

ATTACKS:
- Unarmed Strike (Melee, 5▲ Knockdown, Size 1H, Non-Lethal)
- Phaser type-2 (Ranged, 7▲, Size 1H, Charge)

SPECIAL RULES:
- **By the Book:** When engaged in Social Conflict with Player Characters over Starfleet orders, protocols, or

procedures, if Nechayev buys any additional d20s, she may re-roll a single d20.

- **Point of Order:** When Nechayev assists another character using her Diplomacy Focus, she may re-roll her d20.
- **Understands the Cardassians:** When negotiating with Cardassians, Nechayev reduces the Difficulty of all Tasks by 1, to a minimum of 1.
- **Menacing**

VICE ADMIRAL JAMES LEYTON [MAJOR NPC]

Admiral Leyton is the Chief of Starfleet Operations, at Starfleet Headquarters in San Francisco on Earth. He has operational authority over fleet and ship deployments across the entire Federation and beyond but, in practice, this authority is delegated. Vice admirals, rear admirals, and captains operating in particular regions are trusted to have more understanding of their commands and regions.

Leyton is a veteran of several conflicts and police actions, including wars against the Cardassians and the Tzenkethi, and skirmishes with the Romulans, Tholians, and Borg. He is a firm believer in preparing to deal with new threats; he has openly stated his belief that war with the Dominion is inevitable.

He has strong relationships with many officers who served under him earlier in his career. He uses his knowledge of those officers, and his role as Chief of Starfleet Operations, to ensure that each is posted where their skills are most needed.

VALUES:
- Respect the Chain of Command, Whether You Agree with It or Not
- Too Many People Underestimate the Threats We Face
- Protecting the Federation is Paramount
- No Price is Too High for Security

TRAITS: Human, Flag Officer

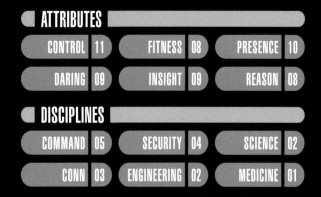

ATTRIBUTES

CONTROL 11	FITNESS 08	PRESENCE 10
DARING 09	INSIGHT 09	REASON 08

DISCIPLINES

COMMAND 05	SECURITY 04	SCIENCE 02
CONN 03	ENGINEERING 02	MEDICINE 01

FOCUSES: Deception, Intelligence Briefings, Military Strategy, Politics, Psychology, Security Policy

STRESS: 12 **RESISTANCE: 0**

ATTACKS:
- Unarmed Strike (Melee, 5⚔ Knockdown, Size 1H, Non-Lethal)
- Phaser type-2 (Ranged, 7⚔, Size 1H, Charge)

SPECIAL RULES:
- **Authoratative:** When involved in a Social Conflict to give or explain orders, or to remain with a course of action when a subordinate officer attempts to persuade him otherwise, if Leyton buys additional dice, he may re-roll any number of d20s in his dice pool.
- **Menacing**
- **Paranoia:** When attempting a Task to detect a threat or peril (personal, to a starship, or politically through intelligence reports), Leyton gains one additional d20 automatically. All such Tasks increase in Complication Range by 1 (to 19-20), and complications may cause Leyton to misjudge the scale of the threat.

TACTICAL CARTOGRAPHY 5-80

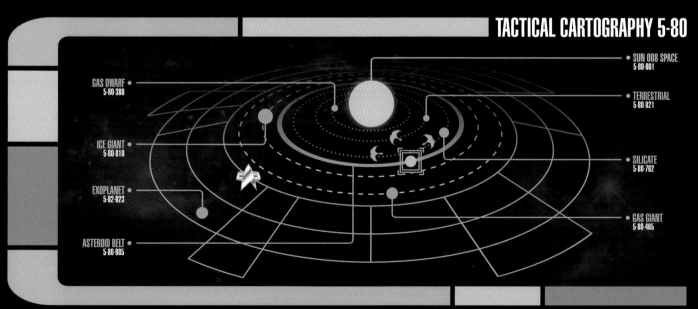

GAS DWARF
5-80-388

ICE GIANT
5-80-810

EXOPLANET
5-82-023

ASTEROID BELT
5-80-985

SUN 008 SPACE
5-80-001

TERRESTRIAL
5-80-821

SILICATE
5-80-762

GAS GIANT
5-80-465

COMMAND PERSONNEL
DIPLOMATS AND DELEGATES

SAREK [MAJOR NPC]

Sarek of Vulcan gave the greater part of his life to the Federation. A scientist, diplomat, ambassador and politician of great wisdom and experience, he served as Vulcan's Ambassador to Earth, a member of the Federation Council, and as representative of the Federation to many worlds.

Those accomplishments are enough for Sarek's name to be spoken with reverence, and his words quoted over decades by those seeking peace. His contributions to the Federation are many, and often subtle, but he left a lasting mark. While proud of his Vulcan heritage he had an appreciation of humanity, and both of his marriages were to human women.

In 2366, at the age of 201, Sarek was diagnosed with Bendii syndrome. This neurological disorder afflicts elderly Vulcans, impairing their emotional control and broadcasting their emotions telepathically. His condition was stabilized through a mind-meld with Captain Picard so that he could continue his last diplomatic work. He retired to Vulcan shortly afterwards. He died in 2368, survived by his second wife and the younger of his two sons, Spock. His eldest son, Sybok, had died some 80 years earlier.

VALUES:
- What is Necessary is Never Unwise
- My Logic is Uncertain Where My Son is Concerned
- Proud of the Vulcan Way

TRAITS: Vulcan, Legendary Diplomat

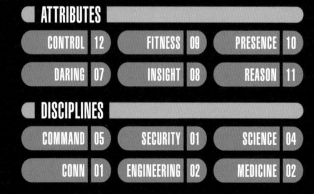

ATTRIBUTES
| CONTROL | 12 | FITNESS | 09 | PRESENCE | 10 |
| DARING | 07 | INSIGHT | 08 | REASON | 11 |

DISCIPLINES
| COMMAND | 05 | SECURITY | 01 | SCIENCE | 04 |
| CONN | 01 | ENGINEERING | 02 | MEDICINE | 02 |

FOCUSES: Astrophysics, Composure, Diplomacy, History, Politics, Vulcan Philosophy

STRESS: 10   **RESISTANCE:** 0

ATTACKS:
- Nerve Pinch (Melee, 5$\blacktriangle$ Intense, Size 1H, Non-lethal)

SPECIAL RULES:
- **Bendii Syndrome:** This rule applies only to Sarek in games set in the 2360s. Sarek has +2 Complication Range on all Tasks that involve social interaction and control of his emotions. Additionally, Sarek loses the Composure Focus. These penalties can be removed for the duration of a scene if a psychic character succeeds at a **Difficulty 3 Control + Medicine Task**; they can be removed for the remainder of a mission if Sarek can perform a mind-meld with someone suitably disciplined and orderly (Gamemaster's discretion), though this can have massive side-effects for the recipient of the Meld (Gamemaster's discretion again).
- **Cold Reading** (Talent)
- **Mind-meld** (Talent)
- **Nerve Pinch** (Talent)
- **Renowned Diplomat:** Sarek's renown and reputation are such that his mere presence

Sarek's role in Federation history is a long and important one, and it allows him to turn up in a wide range of stories and missions.

IN THE ORIGINAL SERIES ERA

In his prime, Sarek either represents Vulcan within the Federation or represents the Federation to outsiders. He has such prominence in political and diplomatic matters that many notable diplomats worked as his aides or attachés, or studied his achievements during their training. He is accustomed to the intricacies of national and international politics, and operates amongst the highest levels of government, dealing with heads of state and ambassadors. Any mission involving him will be of considerable importance to Vulcan or the whole Federation. Towards the end of this era, Sarek is instrumental in making treaties with the Klingon Empire, including the earliest forms of the Khitomer Accords in the 2290s. This is one of the rare occasions when he worked directly with his son, Spock.

Sarek is stubborn, stoic, and extremely controlled, almost the archetypical Vulcan in many ways. He doesn't have much time for frivolity, or anything he regards as wasteful or unnecessary. This may cause difficulties with more reckless or emotional crews, though not so much as to hinder any task at hand.

IN THE NEXT GENERATION ERA

In the years leading up to his death in 2368, Sarek's reputation is such that, even while relatively inactive due to age and infirmity, his work is always of considerable importance. One of his great accomplishments in 2366 is diplomatic talks with the reclusive Legarans, something that had taken nearly a century to complete. Sarek had overseen these talks personally from the outset. If Sarek is present in person during a negotiation, he will endeavor to be much as he once was in earlier times. There are limits to his control even with the assistance of his staff. His infirmity and advanced age mean that his presence should be used sparingly, though the effects of his long and distinguished career can be much more evident. In games set after Sarek's death, the impact of his work can be felt in diplomatic missions involving people who studied under him, or worlds he visited during his own missions.

---

can serve as the groundwork for diplomatic talks. Once per scene, when a character is involved in a Social Conflict reflecting peace talks, negotiations, or some other diplomatic mission, they may re-roll a single d20 as long as Sarek is present in the scene or was instrumental in establishing the talks.

CURZON DAX [MAJOR NPC]

Curzon Dax was the seventh host of the Dax symbiont and best known for his service as Federation Ambassador to the Klingon Empire. Before that his efforts in the creation and ratification of peace treaties between the Federation and the Klingons were notable. Curzon was, famously, a gambler and womanizer, known for his unorthodox approaches to challenging situations, and his enthusiasms for other cultures. Indeed, his love of the good life was such that it is surprising that he managed to accomplish as much as he did.

Continuing a tradition begun by an earlier Dax host, Curzon served as a field docent at the Trill Symbiosis Commission, continuing the Dax reputation for 'breaking' initiates who did not meet his standards. His long life allowed him to meet a great many important people: he studied under Sarek of Vulcan; established a lasting friendship with the Klingons Kor, Koloth, and Kang; and encountered many Starfleet officers at various stages in their careers, from Captain Hikaru Sulu of the *Excelsior* to being a friend and mentor to a young Benjamin Sisko.

Curzon died in 2367, over a century old, after over-exerting himself seeking *jamaharon* on Risa, a testament to a long life lived to the fullest. His memories and experiences live on in Lieutenant Jadzia Dax, a Starfleet officer serving aboard Deep Space 9.

VALUES:
- Life is Meant to Be Lived
- Hold Yourself and Others to the Highest Standards
- Sometimes, a Dax doesn't think; They Just Act
- Godfather and Namesake of the Son of Kang

TRAITS: Trill, Dax Symbiont, Honored Amongst the Klingons

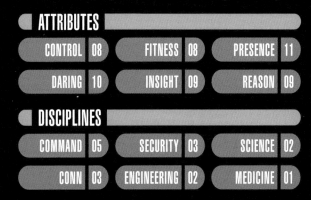

ATTRIBUTES

CONTROL	08	FITNESS	08	PRESENCE	11
DARING	10	INSIGHT	09	REASON	09

DISCIPLINES

COMMAND	05	SECURITY	03	SCIENCE	02
CONN	03	ENGINEERING	02	MEDICINE	01

FOCUSES: Cultural Studies, Diplomacy, Intimidation, Gambler, Persuasion, Trill Symbiosis

STRESS: 11   **RESISTANCE:** 0

CURZON DAX IN PLAY

Curzon Dax has been involved in numerous notable events and, present or not, he may have an impact on events.

IN THE ORIGINAL SERIES ERA

Curzon received the Dax symbiont in 2285 and studied diplomacy during his 20s both before and after his joining. He was noticed around this time, as he was a key negotiator during talks with the Klingons. In this capacity, Curzon's notoriety in both the Federation and amongst the Klingons is assured. In the later decades of the era, almost any non-aggressive contact between the Federation and the Klingons is liable to involve, or at least mention Dax, especially after the Khitomer Accords in 2293.

Curzon's lust for life and his hot-headed, stubborn manner can make him somewhat troublesome to work with, with a share of problems. Curzon, though, has a knack for finding opportunities in those problems, and he makes friends easily, especially with those who care less about rules and more about results.

IN THE NEXT GENERATION ERA

Dax's successes and many years as Federation Ambassador to the Klingon Empire, made Curzon a significant figure in the Federation's diplomatic circles. He would often be called to open talks with newly-discovered cultures and mediate disputes between known cultures. These activities often required the support of a starship and crew. In these missions, Dax came into contact with many people, from all walks of life.

After his death in 2367, the impact of his life can be felt in the peace with the Klingons, and in people he guided and advised during his lengthy career. In his later years, Curzon's lust for life is not lessened, though his experience meant that he could mitigate the problems his recklessness caused.

KNOWLEDGE OF THE TRILL

Curzon Dax is a widely-known, perhaps notorious, figure. This is something which seems at odds with the little knowledge outsiders have of the Trill and their symbiotic nature. The Trill are not particularly secretive, but they don't go out of their way to advertise which individuals are joined and which are not. As only a tiny proportion of Trill are joined, this means that most people can go their entire lives without meeting a joined Trill. The ones do meet a joined Trill might never realize it.

ATTACKS:
- Unarmed Strike (Melee, 4⚔ Knockdown, Size 1H, Non-lethal)

SPECIAL RULES:
- **Advisor** (Talent)
- **Collaboration (Command)** (Talent)
- **Ebullient and Reckless:** Curzon is impulsive and prone to excess, but these qualities have brought him success after success. His charisma and infectious enthusiasm help him form lasting and meaningful relationships, both professionally and personally even though they have also gotten Curzon into more than his fair share of trouble over the years. When attempting a Task during a Social Conflict, Curzon may choose to suffer a Complication in addition to the results of the Task. If he does this, he gains one additional d20 on the Task. The limit of three additional d20s applies as normal.
- **Joined:** Curzon is host to the Dax symbiont. Once per mission, he may gain one additional Focus for the duration of the current scene, representing experiences and skills from past Dax hosts.

AMBASSADOR LWAXANA TROI [MAJOR NPC]

"Memorable" is a polite description of Lwaxana Troi. She is a woman with larger-than-life flamboyance and hardly what most people imagine a diplomat to be but, once met, she is seldom forgotten. Her flirtatious manner often leaves people flustered or embarrassed, while her blunt honesty and her telepathy mean that few people can hide anything from her. These talents are employed to cut through formality to reach the heart of a matter, or sometimes just for amusement.

Daughter of a noble house, Lwaxana Troi has served as an ambassador for Betazed, and the Federation as a whole. Her unorthodox and outlandish manner has helped create lasting treaties and agreements in many situations and with many diverse cultures. Her status as Federation Ambassador involves her in a wide variety of different situations, bringing her into contact with many different people from all walks of life.

She is fiercely protective of her family, and especially her daughter, Deanna. She feels the same about anyone she considers a friend, and she makes friends easily. As someone who prides herself on brutal honesty she often seems reluctant to take things seriously. Whether this is part of the way she carries herself, or true part of her nature is, and should remain, bit of a mystery.

Ambassador Troi is routinely accompanied by her laconic valet, Mr. Homn.

VALUES:

- Daughter of the Fifth House, Holder of the Sacred Chalice of Rixx, and Heir to the Holy Rings of Betazed
- Do Not Be What Others Expect of You
- Life's True Gift is the Capacity to Enjoy Enjoyment
- What Matters the Most is Company

TRAITS: Betazoid

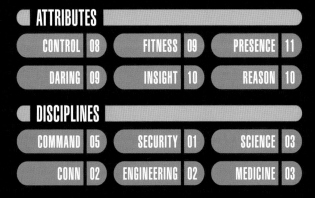

ATTRIBUTES

CONTROL	08	FITNESS	09	PRESENCE	11
DARING	09	INSIGHT	10	REASON	10

DISCIPLINES

COMMAND	05	SECURITY	01	SCIENCE	03
CONN	02	ENGINEERING	02	MEDICINE	03

FOCUSES: Betazoid Culture, Cultural Studies, Etiquette, Persuasion, Psychology, Politics

STRESS: 10　　**RESISTANCE:** 0

ATTACKS:

- Unarmed Strike (Melee, 2⚔ Knockdown, Size 1H, Non-lethal)

SPECIAL RULES:

- **Telepath (Talent)**

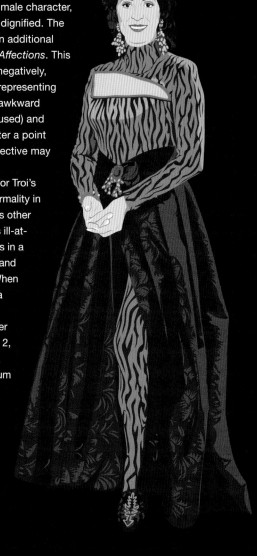

- **Object of Affection:** When she first appears in a mission, Lwaxana Troi may select a single Player Character or NPC to be the object of her affections for that mission. She will typically choose an older male character, often someone quiet and dignified. The chosen character gains an additional Directive: *Lwaxana Troi's Affections*. This is most likely to be used negatively, creating a Complication (representing some embarrassment or awkward situation Mrs. Troi has caused) and giving the chosen character a point of Determination. This Directive may not be Challenged.
- **Break the Ice:** Ambassador Troi's manner breaks through formality in a way that sometimes puts other diplomats and negotiators ill-at-ease. It does open up talks in a way that proper etiquette and procedure often do not. When attempting a Task during a Social Conflict, Lwaxana may choose to increase her Complication Range by 1, 2, or 3. If the Task succeeds, she gains bonus Momentum equal to the amount by which she increased her Complication range.
- **Diplomatic Expertise:** Whenever Ambassador Troi attempts a Task within a Social Conflict and buys one or more additional dice, she may re-roll her dice pool.

LWAXANA TROI IN PLAY

Lwaxana Troi is active in Federation politics and diplomacy during the late 24th century, and can crop up in many places and situations. Her high status as a Betazoid noble, a Betazoid representative to the Federation, and a Federation representative, gives her all the excuses she needs to travel visit many cultures.

She can therefore appear as part of almost any diplomatic mission: alone, accompanied by Mr. Homn, or in a Federation delegation. She's liable to be disruptive to mission, providing fuel for all kinds of side antics and complications to the main story. She will ingratiate herself with or embarrass the crew (or both). If she finds someone she particularly likes, because she enjoys their company, or because it's amusing when they become flustered, she may return from time to time.

As frustrating as Lwaxana might be to the orderly running of a starship, she is an insightful negotiator and a skilled diplomat. She has extensive knowledge of politics and other cultures, and she can often help bring resolution where problems have seemed insurmountable. She will leverage social and political power, or simply shock everyone into a solution because of her unorthodox approach.

DIPLOMAT [NOTABLE NPC]

Diplomatic functionaries are a natural part of any missions where one world or civilization speaks with another. Starship captains are expected to act as diplomats when necessary but, for long-term talks, a professional is preferable.

VALUES:
Peace can be attained through effort and compromise

TRAITS: Human

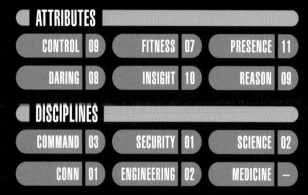

ATTRIBUTES

CONTROL 09	FITNESS 07	PRESENCE 11
DARING 08	INSIGHT 10	REASON 09

DISCIPLINES

COMMAND 03	SECURITY 01	SCIENCE 02
CONN 01	ENGINEERING 02	MEDICINE —

FOCUSES: Diplomacy, Politics, Research

STRESS: 8   **RESISTANCE:** 0

ATTACKS:
- Unarmed Strike (Melee, 2▲ Knockdown, Size 1H, Non-lethal)

SPECIAL RULES:
- Defuse the Tension (Talent)

ATTACHÉ [MINOR NPC]

Attachés are members of a high-ranking diplomat's support staff: advisors, researchers, and assistants. Many attachés have a particular expertise: military (sometimes a retired military officer), legal (a lawyer with appropriate expertise), scientific (a scientist of particular prominence), or trade (an expert in macroeconomics).

TRAITS: Human

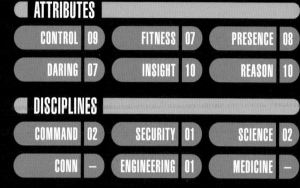

ATTRIBUTES

CONTROL 09	FITNESS 07	PRESENCE 08
DARING 07	INSIGHT 10	REASON 10

DISCIPLINES

COMMAND 02	SECURITY 01	SCIENCE 02
CONN —	ENGINEERING 01	MEDICINE —

STRESS: 8   **RESISTANCE:** 0

ATTACKS:
- Unarmed Strike (Melee, 2▲ Knockdown, Size 1H, Non-lethal)

SPECIAL RULES:
- **Specialist Subject:** An Attaché may be given a specialty, granting them a single Focus (even though Minor NPCs normally cannot have Focuses), and possibly modifying their Disciplines. Focuses are chosen from the following list:

  - **Cultural Attaché:** Gain either *Art* or *Cultural Studies* as a Focus.
  - **Health Attaché:** Gain *Public Health* as a Focus. Increase Medicine to 02, Reduce Science to 01, reduce Security to 00. (Reduce Stress to 7 & Unarmed Strike damage to 1▲.)
  - **Legal Attaché:** Gain *Law* as a Focus.
  - **Military Attaché:** Gain *Military Strategy* or *Military Protocol* as a Focus. Increase Security to 02, reduce Science to 01. (Increase Stress to 9 & Unarmed Strike damage to 3▲.)
  - **Press Attaché:** Gain *Journalism* or *Public Relations* as a Focus.
  - **Science Attaché:** Gain a single field of Scientific study as a Focus.
  - **Trade Attaché:** Gain *Economics* as a Focus.

MODIFYING NPCS

The Notable and Minor NPCs in this section are generic, allowing the Gamemaster to adjust them for different situations. This allows these characters to be used as people from Federation worlds or other civilizations, depending on the needs of the game.

Here the NPCs are listed as human, and Attributes have been increased due to species (in the case of humans, any three.) To change the character's species, change the character's species Trait, reduce the three highest Attributes by one each, and then apply the new species' Attribute modifiers. At this stage, it may also be appropriate to change the character's Values, adjust Focuses to suit the chosen culture, or add any appropriate Talents or special rules for the species (such as a Betazoid's telepathy, or a Klingon's *brak'lul*).

NEGOTIATOR [MINOR NPC]

Diplomacy is the responsibility of diplomats and ambassadors but they cannot do the job alone. They will normally be accompanied by a staff of aides, assistants, and negotiators of lower rank. Subordinate negotiators often handle individual sessions in a larger set of talks, negotiating the nitty-gritty of individual treaty clauses or details of an agenda.

TRAITS: Human

ATTRIBUTES

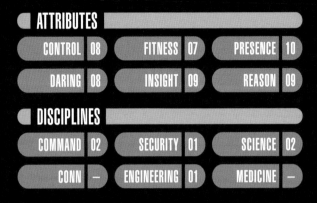

CONTROL 08	FITNESS 07	PRESENCE 10
DARING 08	INSIGHT 09	REASON 09

DISCIPLINES

COMMAND 02	SECURITY 01	SCIENCE 02
CONN —	ENGINEERING 01	MEDICINE —

FOCUSES: Negotiation

STRESS: 8   **RESISTANCE:** 0

ATTACKS:
- Unarmed Strike (Melee, 2▲ Knockdown, Size 1H, Non-lethal)

SPECIAL RULES:
- Focused Training: Negotiators have a single Focus, even though they are Minor NPCs.

CHAPTER
6.30

COMMAND PERSONNEL
STARFLEET PERSONNEL

PATHFINDER SPECIALIST [NOTABLE NPC]

Across the Galaxy, there are regions of space that are difficult to navigate. The Delphic Expanse, home to the Xindi and rife with spatial anomalies is one such example; the Badlands, often used by Maquis raiders to evade pursuit, is another. These regions, as well as border and frontier regions of space, are difficult and dangerous to travel, and possess numerous unknown hazards that could destroy a ship.

A pathfinder — not a formal title — is an expert at navigating these uncharted regions safely. Their expertise allows them to map dangerous or unexplored space, making subsequent voyages easier and safer. Elite pilots with this kind of skill are often a valuable resource for an Admiral, to be deployed as and when needed. They are often assigned to scout and reconnaissance vessels and sent on long-range exploratory missions.

VALUES:
- The First to See Those Stars Up Close

TRAITS: Human

ATTRIBUTES

| CONTROL | 11 | FITNESS | 08 | PRESENCE | 07 |
| DARING | 10 | INSIGHT | 08 | REASON | 10 |

DISCIPLINES

| COMMAND | 02 | SECURITY | 01 | SCIENCE | 02 |
| CONN | 03 | ENGINEERING | 01 | MEDICINE | 01 |

FOCUSES: Astronavigation, Helm Operations

STRESS: 9   **RESISTANCE:** 0

ATTACKS:
- Unarmed Strike (Melee, 2▲ Knockdown, Size 1H, Non-lethal)
- Phaser type-1 (Ranged, 3▲, Size 1H, Charge, Hidden 1)

SPECIAL RULES:
- **Find the Path:** If the pathfinder specialist buys one or more additional d20s when attempting a Task to navigate or chart a difficult or dangerous region of space, they may re-roll a single d20. During any Extended Task attempt to navigate through a perilous region of space, a Pathfinder Specialist (or a character assisted by a Pathfinder Specialist), gains *Scrutinize 2* when rolling Challenge Dice.

ACADEMY INSTRUCTOR [NOTABLE NPC]

Starfleet Academy requires a large number of instructors, and drawn from officers and enlisted personnel across Starfleet. Many distinguished officers have spent a year or two teaching classes at the Academy, often while between more active or dangerous postings. The really good officers see it as an opportunity to pass on what they have experienced.

VALUES:
- There's Nothing as Important as Shaping the Next Generation

TRAITS: Human

ATTRIBUTES

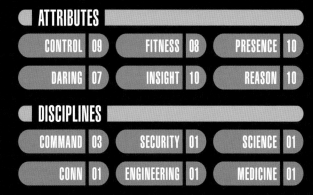

| CONTROL | 09 | FITNESS | 08 | PRESENCE | 10 |
| DARING | 07 | INSIGHT | 10 | REASON | 10 |

DISCIPLINES

| COMMAND | 03 | SECURITY | 01 | SCIENCE | 01 |
| CONN | 01 | ENGINEERING | 01 | MEDICINE | 01 |

FOCUSES: Teaching

STRESS: 9   **RESISTANCE:** 0

ATTACKS:
- Unarmed Strike (Melee, 2▲ Knockdown, Size 1H, Non-lethal)
- Phaser type-2 (Ranged, 4▲, Size 1H, Charge)

SPECIAL RULES:
- **Teacher:** Choose a single Discipline other than Command, and increase it by 1. Then select a single Focus to represent the subject taught by the Academy Instructor.
- **Collaboration (Talent):** Choose a single Discipline for this Talent.

CADET [MINOR NPC]

The next generation of Starfleet officers can be found both at Starfleet Academy, and on field assignments ("cadet cruises") aboard starships and starbases. This gives them practical experience while they continue studying. A little over-eager to please their superiors, with rules and regulations at their fingertips, cadets need guidance as they become young officers.

The profile below represents a Command Track cadet. For cadets in other tracks, adjust the Disciplines accordingly.

TRAITS: Human

ATTRIBUTES

CONTROL 09	FITNESS 09	PRESENCE 08
DARING 08	INSIGHT 09	REASON 08

DISCIPLINES

COMMAND 02	SECURITY 01	SCIENCE —
CONN 02	ENGINEERING 01	MEDICINE —

STRESS: 10   **RESISTANCE:** 0

ATTACKS:
- Unarmed Strike (Melee, 2▲ Knockdown, Size 1H, Non-lethal)
- Phaser type-1 (Ranged, 4▲, Size 1H, Charge, Hidden 1)

SPECIAL RULES:
- Untapped Potential (Talent)

JAG OFFICER [NOTABLE NPC]

As part of the Judge Advocate General's office, this officer is especially knowledgeable about the law. In most situations, a JAG Officer provides legal advice to Starfleet personnel, especially commanding officers, in their assigned region or facility. They also serve as prosecuting and defense counsels during courts-martial, and as judges during inquiries, hearings, and courts-martial. JAGs can judge or advise on civilian matters as well, particularly where a ruling may affect (or serve as precedent for) Starfleet operations, or in frontier regions where Starfleet is the established Federation presence.

VALUES:
- Law is the Foundation Upon Which an Orderly Society is Built

TRAITS: Human

ATTRIBUTES

CONTROL 09	FITNESS 07	PRESENCE 10
DARING 08	INSIGHT 09	REASON 11

DISCIPLINES

COMMAND 03	SECURITY 02	SCIENCE 02
CONN 01	ENGINEERING 01	MEDICINE 01

FOCUSES: History, Law, Rhetoric

STRESS: 9   **RESISTANCE:** 0

ATTACKS:
- Unarmed Strike (Melee, 3▲ Knockdown, Size 1H, Non-lethal)
- Phaser type-1 (Ranged, 4▲, Size 1H, Charge, Hidden 1)

SPECIAL RULES:
- **Jurisprudence:** The JAG Officer is extremely well-versed in the theory and philosophy of law, and may re-roll one d20 on a Task that uses the character's Reason and their Law Focus.
- **Advisor (Talent)**
- **Threatening 3**

COMMAND PERSONNEL
SUPPORTING CHARACTERS

OVERVIEW

This section provides a varied selection of interesting supporting characters that can be introduced during an ongoing game especially those specialized in the Command or Conn Disciplines.

They are all built using the supporting characters rules on page 134 of the *Star Trek Adventures* core rulebook. Each one is accompanied by notes on how that character might be customized when reintroduced in later missions.

None of the Supporting Characters include character species effects. In cases where a different species is needed, add a Trait related to the character's species, and increase the character's Attributes accordingly. The most straightforward option is to use Human as the default character species, adding the Trait "Human", and increasing any three Attributes by +1.

DIPLOMATIC AIDE

This Supporting Character is a specialist in negotiations and serves as a junior officer in the Diplomatic Corps. They're well-versed in psychology, politics and the art of rhetoric, though they may have little practical diplomatic experience in the field. They are more valuable as assistants and advisors rather than as leaders in any talks.

ATTRIBUTES

CONTROL 09	FITNESS 07	PRESENCE 09
DARING 08	INSIGHT 10	REASON 08

DISCIPLINES

COMMAND 04	SECURITY 01	SCIENCE 03
CONN 02	ENGINEERING 02	MEDICINE 01

FOCUSES: Diplomacy, Politics, Psychology

STRESS: 8   RESISTANCE: 0

ATTACKS:
- Unarmed Strike (Melee, 2🅐 Knockdown, Size 1H, Non-lethal)
- Phaser type-1 (Ranged, 4🅐, Size 1H, Charge, Hidden 1)

USE AND DEVELOPMENT

The Diplomatic Aide can be useful in support of officers in the middle of negotiations or diplomatic missions. While all Starfleet officers are expected to have some diplomatic training, the aide's specialized training makes them valuable to those who have other skills.

- SPECIES: Aside from humans, Betazoids, Denobulans, and Trill are very useful diplomatic aides, due to their keen social awareness.

- Rank: The character will probably be a Lieutenant (junior grade) or full Lieutenant. Ensigns are unlikely to have specialized in diplomacy, and there are few enlisted personnel within that Starfleet department.

- Values: A Value that helps the character during negotiations, such as a fervent belief in peaceful resolutions, can be useful. The character does need to have another way to gain Determination, such as being given it by the Commanding Officer, or a second Value that can generate complications.

- Attributes: Insight (reading people and situations), Presence (commanding attention), or Reason (thoughtful analysis) are all useful Attributes to increase.

- Disciplines: Command is the obvious choice to increase here, but Security (wariness in dangerous situations; familiarity with military and defense treaties) and Science (understanding of subjects such as psychology; or theories behind politics, economics, and decision making) are useful too.

- FOCUSES: Additional Focuses can give the character a broad skill base and allow them to engage in a range of situations. Focuses like *Cultural Studies* or *Law* can expand the character's work.

- **Talents:** As an advisor and assistant the talents *Advisor* and *Collaboration* are especially useful, whether or not the character is being directly controlled.

EVA SPECIALIST

This Supporting Character has worked in unusual environments, especially hard vacuum low- and micro-gravity conditions. Zero-G training is a standard course at Starfleet Academy for any officer operating outside of a Class M environment (commonly Conn and Operations personnel), but some individuals take to Zero-G particularly well. These specialists reliably perform complex extra-vehicular activities such as repair and maintenance work outside the ship. Tasks such as replacing damaged hull plating and other external components require considerable physical conditioning.

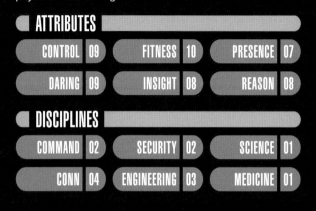

ATTRIBUTES

CONTROL 09	FITNESS 10	PRESENCE 07
DARING 09	INSIGHT 08	REASON 08

DISCIPLINES

COMMAND 02	SECURITY 02	SCIENCE 01
CONN 04	ENGINEERING 03	MEDICINE 01

FOCUSES: Athletics, Extra-Vehicular Activities, Repairs and Maintenance

STRESS: 12   **RESISTANCE:** 02 (EVA Suit)

ATTACKS:
- Unarmed Strike (Melee, 3⚔ Knockdown, Size 1H, Non-lethal)
- Phaser type-1 (Ranged, 4⚔, Size 1H, Charge, Hidden 1)

USE AND DEVELOPMENT
The EVA Specialist is a good option for an alternative character in situations where a player's main character is unsuited to the activities at hand. Their skill in an unusual and specialized field makes them extremely useful in certain situations.

- **Species:** Aside from humans, Tellarites and Vulcans have the conditioning and precision to excel as EVA Specialists.

- **Rank:** The character may be a junior officer such as an Ensign or Lieutenant (junior grade) with a natural gift for EVA work, or they may be an NCO such as a Yeoman/Specialist or similar.

BETAZOID SUPPORTING CHARACTERS

Unlike most other species, Betazoid characters are required to take one of their species' Talents. This conflicts with the Supporting Character rules, as a brand-new Supporting Character does not normally have Talents.

In this situation, a new Betazoid Supporting Character has no Talents. The character is assumed to have some unknown level of empathic or telepathic ability. Naturally, the character "knows", but it's unknown to everyone else because it hasn't appeared in the game.

When reintroducing the same Betazoid character in subsequent missions, one of the Talents selected for the character must be one of the Betazoid species Talents. It doesn't matter if it was the first Talent selected, or the fourth, as long as one of them a Betazoid Talent.

This applies to a Supporting Character from any species with one or more mandatory Talents.

- **Values:** The character's Values are likely to reflect their dedication and certainty: working on a starship hull is not for those with weak stomachs or self-doubt.

- **Attributes:** Control (precision tasks), Daring (taking risks and making quick decisions in peril), and Fitness (physical conditioning) are all useful Attributes to increase.

- **Disciplines:** Conn is the obvious Discipline to increase here, but Engineering (covering technical activities) is a valuable one. Increasing Security expands the character's possible role, with zero-G combat training being potentially useful for some crews.

- **Focuses:** Additional Focuses provide the character with a skill base and make them useful in more situations. *Small Craft* allows the character to switch between shuttle and environment suit easily, while a Focus in a particular ship system makes repair work on that system easier. Combat-related Focuses, as well as Focuses like *Infiltration*, can make the character invaluable during battle.

- **Talents:** The Spacewalk talent (page 50) is a natural first choice here, and *Precision Maneuvering* can be helpful if moving quickly through debris fields or other dense terrain. Beyond that, Talent choices should reflect the character's working life.

JUNIOR BRIDGE OFFICER

There are normally a few young officers regularly stationed on the bridge, either running the bridge stations or standing by to relieve another officer at one of those positions. Normally they are the relief when the flight controller, operations manager, or tactical officer is called to a briefing, away mission, or some other urgent assignment. This gives these characters first-hand experience of bridge operations, and allows them to witness command decisions being made, while their role ensures that vital positions on the bridge are always manned.

ATTRIBUTES

CONTROL 10	FITNESS 07	PRESENCE 09
DARING 08	INSIGHT 08	REASON 09

DISCIPLINES

COMMAND 02	SECURITY 02	SCIENCE 01
CONN 04	ENGINEERING 03	MEDICINE 01

FOCUSES: Astronavigation, Helm Operations, Power Management

STRESS: 9   **RESISTANCE:** 0

ATTACKS:
- Unarmed Strike (Melee, 3▲ Knockdown, Size 1H, Non-lethal)
- Phaser type-1 (Ranged, 4▲, Size 1H, Charge, Hidden 1)

USE AND DEVELOPMENT

Junior bridge officers are invaluable but also invisible. No starship bridge position can be left empty, at least one junior should be nearby to step in whenever a Main Character leaves their station. This may not have much of an impact most of the time but, if the ship finds itself in an emergency while the main Flight Controller is on an away mission, introducing a Junior Bridge Officer helps fill that vital role.

- **Species:** Aside from humans, Andorians, Bajorans, Tellarites, Trill and Vulcans all tend towards precision and certainty, making them effective junior bridge officers.

- **Rank:** The character is likely to be someone on their first posting, an Ensign or a Lieutenant (junior grade).

- **Values:** Dedication to Starfleet and the desire to succeed are vital on a starship bridge, as there is little room for uncertainty at the controls.

- **Attributes:** Control (precision and a methodical approach), Daring (decisive action in a crisis), and Reason (analyzing and interpreting new information effectively) are all useful Attributes to increase.

- **Disciplines:** Conn is the obvious option to increase here if the character spends much of their time at the helm, but Security (operating weapons and other defensive systems), Engineering (control of internal systems) and Science (operating probes and sensor systems) are useful too.

- **Focuses:** Additional Focuses can provide the character with a broad skill base and let them contribute in many situations. A character might select *Tactical Systems* to help them operate the ship's weapons more effectively, or *Sensor Suites* to aid in surveys and scanning for trouble.

- **Talents:** As juniors often take over at the helm, the *Multi-Tasking Talent* can be quite valuable. Depending on the stations for which they are best-suited, *Pack Tactics* or *Technical Expertise* may also be useful.

LEGAL COUNSEL

Federation laws, codes and regulations are complex and, even within the narrower field of Starfleet regulations, allowances for diverse cultures have to be made. Command personnel and others need some discretion in many challenging circumstances. This makes a complex legal system. Officers are expected to have a broad understanding of regulations; commanding officers should have more detailed knowledge. Even so, specialists with a deep knowledge of law and precedent are often necessary. A larger starship or starbase may have a small legal staff to advise personnel of their rights and responsibilities, and to assist them if they have testify at a hearing or face a court martial. Smaller vessels may lack such specialized personnel, but they are only a subspace communique away.

ATTRIBUTES

CONTROL 08	FITNESS 07	PRESENCE 10
DARING 08	INSIGHT 09	REASON 09

DISCIPLINES

COMMAND 04	SECURITY 02	SCIENCE 02
CONN 03	ENGINEERING 01	MEDICINE 01

FOCUSES: Debate, Law, Starfleet Protocols

STRESS: 9   **RESISTANCE:** 0

ATTACKS:

- Unarmed Strike (Melee, 3⚔ Knockdown, Size 1H, Non-lethal)
- Phaser type-1 (Ranged, 4⚔, Size 1H, Charge, Hidden 1)

USE AND DEVELOPMENT

Legal Counsel can serve well as an alternate character speaking on another character's behalf, or as an assistant providing advice and guidance. They won't appear often, but their specialized knowledge means that it will be obvious when they are needed to offer legal advice. Missions that focus on moral or ethical matters, how these interact a Starfleet officer's duty, and whether actions fall within the law, are likely to involve Legal Counsel.

- **Species:** Aside from Humans, Betazoids, Tellarites, Trill, and Vulcans, all have an aptitude for the attention to detail needed for legal work.

- **Rank:** The character is likely to be of relatively high rank, often a Lieutenant, or Lieutenant Commander (even though Supporting Characters are not normally of high rank).

- **Values:** Values that reflect the importance of order, or the virtues of truth, are common amongst those in the legal profession.

- **Attributes:** Insight (reading people and situations), Presence (commanding attention), or Reason (thoughtful analysis) are all useful Attributes to increase.

- **Disciplines:** Command is the obvious option to increase here, but Security (experience in interrogation and investigative techniques) and Science (understanding of subjects such as psychology, or a knowledge of forensic sciences) are useful too.

- **Focuses:** Additional Focuses give the character more utility. Focuses like *Cultural Studies* can expand breadth of legal knowledge; an understanding of *History* provides valuable context for precedents; and *Interrogation* can help the character deal with witnesses, or carry out an investigation.

- **Talents:** *Collaboration* is a useful talent when providing legal advice to another character, and *Studious* or *Cold Reading* can be useful talents to have.

SHUTTLE PILOT

Any starship or starbase will have at least a complement of support craft and, while most shuttlecraft are advanced enough that the pilot can set a course and let the computer do the rest of the work, this is not enough in many situations.

Most ships and facilities have a small cadre of dedicated pilots, who operate shuttles and other small craft. These pilots have additional training to allow them to operate effectively away from a starship or base for longer periods, such as if their craft is disabled.

ATTRIBUTES

CONTROL 10	FITNESS 08	PRESENCE 07
DARING 09	INSIGHT 09	REASON 08

DISCIPLINES

COMMAND 01	SECURITY 02	SCIENCE 02
CONN 04	ENGINEERING 03	MEDICINE 01

FOCUSES: Communications Systems, Small Craft, Survival

STRESS: 10   **RESISTANCE:** 0

ATTACKS:
- Unarmed Strike (Melee, 3⊠ Knockdown, Size 1H, Non-lethal)
- Phaser type-2 (Ranged, 5⊠, Size 1H, Charge)

USE AND DEVELOPMENT
The uses of a shuttle pilot should be fairly obvious: operating a shuttle under stressful or dangerous conditions can require a specialist; and a skilled pilot can be of massive help during a crisis. They are more often than not a replacement or alternative character, rather than an assistant.

- **Species:** Aside from Humans, Andorians and Bajorans have the right mix of precision and decisive risk-taking to thrive as pilots.

- **Rank:** Some shuttle pilots are Ensigns and Lieutenants (junior grade), while others are enlisted, and normally Specialist/Yeoman or Chief Specialist rank.

- **Values:** A pilot may have Values that reflect a desire for adventure and a will to face the unknown, strengthening them in the crisis situations where their skills are most useful.

- **Attributes:** Control and Daring are the most useful Attributes for a shuttle pilot to increase, followed by Fitness (moving through, and enduring in, harsh environments) or Reason (diagnosing shuttle problems).

- **Disciplines:** Conn is the most obvious option to improve here, but both Engineering (dealing with technical issues) and Security (dealing with hostiles and similar perils) are good alternatives.

- **Focuses:** Additional Focuses help the character be useful in more situations. Focuses like *Extra-Vehicular Activity* help the character to operate outside a shuttle, while *Atmospheric Operations* is a good choice for pilots who favor flying over planets.

- **Talents:** Regardless of whether the character is serving as an alternative or an assistant, *Precision Maneuvering* or *Push the Limits* are good options, reducing the difficulty of common Tasks in adverse conditions. For more active shuttle pilots, *Fly-By* can be a useful way to maximize the character's impact in an action scene.

SHUTTLECRAFT ("GALILEO SEVEN") C.2267

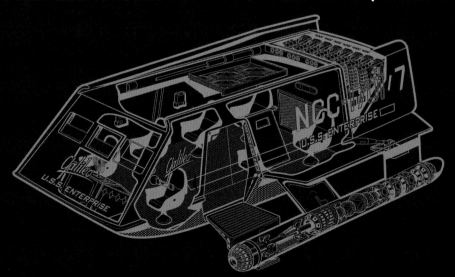

REGISTRY NUMBER NCC-1701/7

ONLINE

LCARS COMMAND INTERFACE READY

LCARS 96-2573

230-681

6865128121 675   3787   2568413   486   87312000 46933 652   5126
4896219865 486   681   0122   682   56842156 96585 863   49833   469-600   351-891
7821231692 198   38704   976210024 198   82500369 12548 268   04589604
0982302058 331   57896   126872258 775   12578952 78546 765   36587451

SYSTEMS

9874321068 963 09840
7920 256 65408
966333 741 07895
32165 524 969

ACCESS GRANTED

6219876954 369 1190
02498763 458 884
6802
36936574 987 7962
287278241 321 41166
MODE SELECT   MODE
159517357 458 46882
7390-4504
798621 963 1089
DECK 10 SECTION 7 CONSOLE 54 ADGE ONLINE
9354477856 159 68712
VISITOR LEVEL TWO CLEARANCE RECOGNIZED
58550322 753 556
SECURITY PROTOCOLS IN PLACE
06858756 852 21080
PLEASE REPORT MALFUNCTIONS TO THE CHIEF ENGINEER ON DUTY
LCARS
451554 050 LCARS

6802

CONSOLE 54 ADGE

STAR TREK
ADVENTURES

ASSEMBLE THE AWAY TEAM, NUMBER ONE!

32MM MINIATURES
THE NEXT GENERATION

32MM MINIATURES
THE ORIGINAL SERIES

32MM MINIATURES
KLINGON WARBAND

32MM MINIATURES
ROMULAN STRIKE TEAM

ENHANCE YOUR ADVENTURES WITH SETS OF EIGHT 32MM HIGH QUALITY RESIN MINIATURES PLUS GEOMORPHIC FLOOR TILES TO RECREATE SHIPS, SPACE STATIONS, LOST COLONIES, AND ANCIENT RUINS!

The Next Generation Bridge Crew
The Original Series Bridge Crew
Klingon Warband
Romulan Strike Team
Borg Drones
Starfleet Away Team

Star Trek Villains
Starfleet Geomorphic Tiles
Klingon Geomorphic Tiles
Romulan Geomorphic Tiles
Lost Colonies & Ancient Ruins Geomorphic Tiles
Borg Geomorphic Tiles